MARK BRANDON READ

CHOPPER 6

MARK BRANDON READ

CHOPPER 6

A BULLET IN TIME SAVES NINE

JOHN BLAKE

Published by John Blake Publishing Ltd,
3 Bramber Court, 2 Bramber Road,
London W14 9PB, England

www.blake.co.uk

First published in paperback in 2008

ISBN: 978 1 84454 502 5

British Library Cataloguing-in-Publication Data:

A catalogue record for this book is available from the British Library.

Design by www.envydesign.co.uk

Printed in Great Britain by CPI Bookmarque, Croydon, CR0 4TD

1 3 5 7 9 10 8 6 4 2

Papers used by John Blake Publishing are natural, recyclable products made from
wood grown in sustainable forests. The manufacturing processes conform to the
environmental regulations of the country of origin.

Every attempt has been made to contact the relevant copyright-holders, but some
were unobtainable. We would be grateful if the appropriate people could contact us.

CONTENTS

PSYCHOLOGY OF FEAR

THE CALABRIAN CONTRACT

'Ultimately, Chopper is a sad case.'
— John Clark, *LA Times*

'Ecrits en prison, les livres de Chopper sont devenus des best-sellers.'
— *FHM* (France)

'Here's the really scary part: Chopper is fact, not fiction, and he's still alive.'
— Anthony Lane, *New Yorker*

'The tale of a brute and a braggart.'
— *The New Yorker*

'An Australian folk hero.'
— *New York Times*

CHAPTER 1

BLOOD MONEY

They kill for the thrill of the hunt.

WHAT if? What if there was an author who wrote about crime and therefore relied upon death to earn a living?

Like the lawyers, the pickle-nosed judges, the coppers, the social workers, the do-gooders, the do-badders, the drunken journos and the psycho book publishers, the author is a parasite sucking from the world's body of evil.

Luckily, there is a never-ending supply of evil. Don't worry, boys and girls, there is enough out there for all of us.

What if the author was to tell a story about a small crew of professional killers whose weapons and ammo, tactics and strategic thinking were all provided for them by the all-time greatest professional hit man in Australian criminal history? It would be a very hard story to believe.

However, bear in mind two things: one is that the hit man is the author's best, oldest and dearest friend and is also a great reader and lover of books; the other is that a smart reader might notice that there has been a series of underworld murders in Australia that have coincided with the release of certain books.

It follows the same pattern. A month or so before the release of the author's next book, or a month or so after, there would be a high-profile underworld murder. There would be front-page headlines about underworld wars and the press would turn to the author for his comments. Each time there would be a mention of his latest books and the result would be seen in book sales.

He would make a killing ... so to speak.

The theory is that a small crew of kids are recruited. They have been taught and trained by the very best and, like the very best, they will never be detected by police or the media because they don't kill for profit or power. They kill for the thrill of the hunt. The sport. The game.

And now, let the story begin ...

When the crew of three first got together for their first hit in 1997, they were codenamed the Young Americans. Fit, clean-cut, strong, good-looking and from well-to-do families. The right education at the right schools. The right family, and social connections in banking, the stock market and computer science.

All of them made more money in their day jobs than the criminal world had to offer. Then cocaine entered the social lives of their friends and business associates. They then realised that the faces who controlled this modern, up-market cocaine trade were a new American Express style of criminal yuppie – and all men backed by enemies and former enemies of the author. So the Young Americans got together. But how did they get started?

Easy.

They just wrote a letter to the author when he was in prison. The author replied with a phone number. It would change all their lives.

The Young Americans were then able to contact the most shadowy and, in the author's opinion, the greatest hit man in Australia. Within a year, with the master blaster directing the play, the Beach Boys were formed.

They called themselves the Beach Boys because the three young men loved boating, surfing, jet skiing and general beach-going and, when not in Melbourne, they lived a lot of the time on the Gold Coast. Their favourite song being the Beach Boys' 'Let's Go Surfing'. Naturally. The code word over the phone for a killing was 'Surf's Up' or 'Let's Go Surfing'.

Of course, no one really goes out and kills anyone just to help a not-so-struggling author.

The Beach Boys, through their mentor and business manager, who, for the sake of the story, I will call Blue Eyes, take contracts from a wide range of people, for a wide range of reasons.

Perish the thought that the Beach Boys are killing everyone. Blue Eyes himself has his own orders to fulfil, so much so that, in frustration, over the phone he says things like, 'Give us a rest, will ya? I can't kill everyone!' Ha! Ha! Ha!

However, the author was promised that enough murders would be carried out for the author, whom I won't name for legal reasons, to fulfil his literary dream: a tenth book. So, dear readers, join me in yet another adventure into the world of crime. Or to put it another way – Surf's Up!

Remember – the sheer fantastic is never believed. That is why it is so easy to carry out.

The police receive all their information from criminals and, believe it or not, the media, which also gathers information from criminals and police. It's like a ladies' sewing circle, all swapping gossip.

I'm talking about matters strictly underworld. When a criminal identity is killed, it is not a matter the general public can help with, unlike a missing person, a bank robbery, a rape, an abducted child or the murder of some poor little old lady.

A criminal killing is strictly in-house and any and all information has to come from the criminal world. However, knowing this also aids the thinking behind underworld murders in the form of disinformation.

If you fill the media and police full of shit prior to a professional killing and just after, you send both groups into an information spin-out.

Also, if you bring in a hit team from outside the mainstream criminal world, then the criminal world itself has to rely on the media or friendly police for 'inside information'. In other words, no one knows anything, but everyone is pretending to know everything.

It's like a game of poker where you pretend to know when you don't and pretend to be confident when you have no right to be.

Acting on information received from insiders who haven't got the faintest idea themselves, media people tell police their secrets, police tell the media their secrets, all of which is based on bullshit from those who don't know. But sometimes it is more sinister, where the disinformation is salted into the mine by those behind the hit in the first place.

I can think of 15 professional hits in Melbourne that will never be solved and both the police and the media are busy busting their guts trying to sort out the total shit they have been fed.

Many crimes are hard to commit and harder to conceal. But murder is easy if it's handled correctly. Most murders are committed by people in the straight world. The wife has burned the bacon for the 10,000th time so you stab her in the breast bone. You spend $500,000 on home renovations and your idiot husband gets rounded corners on the granite benches and you hit him on the head with a meat tenderiser. Then what? No planning. The police come. You end up in a homicide interview room. You tell a few lies but your heart is not in it. You want to confess. You want the nice policeman to tell you that you're not all that bad, that it wasn't your fault. Then, the next thing you're in the dock at the Supreme Court and you're in the bin for the next 10 or 15 years. That's how it works.

Even most murders involving crooks are the same. Cross words then a body. When the murders are planned, half the time they involve imbeciles. There was the one where they buried the body with lime – but it was the wrong type of lime. And even then the lazy buggers didn't spread it around. They just chucked the bag in the hole.

When they found the body it was preserved and the bag of lime was still there – sitting on his chest.

There was also the case of the idiot who killed a woman and put her in a drum of chemicals to dissolve the body. Good idea, except the chemical was a preservative. They found the body in mint condition (except she was dead). I think the crook is now bottling pickled onions in jail, the stupid, fat Yank.

That is why homicide squads around Australia have clearance rates of around 90 per cent. Because most murderers are stupid and only marginally smarter than their victims – who must, of course, be stupider because they're dead.

The disinformation must be in place before the gun is even loaded. It's the heat-of-the-moment killings that get solved and that men go to jail for. That, or big-mouth maggots bring themselves and their whole crew down. Did anyone mention the Russell Street bombing and the Walsh Street murders?

The rule is that, if you shut up and stay shut up, you won't get locked up.

Here's another tip from someone who knows: stick to the story even if it is a fairy-tale. Even if your fucking mother asks you to tell the real secret, whisper a lie into her ear because sticking with the story is as important as getting rid of the murder weapon.

This is a foolproof tactic because if you don't stick to it you're a fool for giving the police the proof to convict you. After a lifetime – some would say a life sentence – of watching other strategies fail, I've concluded this is the only tactic that works.

You might want to share some secrets with people close to you in the name of business or friendship, but you can never hand over the keys to your heart to anyone because they will surely stab you in it, even if they have to put the knife through your back to do it.

They will be unable to help themselves. Don't you think that Clark Kent wanted to tell someone that he was really Superman? The answer is yes. The hardest thing to keep is a secret and the keepers of secrets are supermen, sometimes super *bad* men who will go to their graves with their headstones reading 'Rest in Peace Clark Kent'.

People want to talk. The great crims are those who don't need the reputation. Tough men don't have to tell other people how tough they are. They know it and that's all that matters. Beware the quiet man – he can be as deadly as he is rare.

Crims are like anyone else. They want to brag or confide to mates. But there is no such thing in the underworld as 'mates'. The police have a network of informers who can't wait to pass on any titbits in exchange for the green light, a blind eye or a sling.

So, if you tell the truth to anyone, you can go to jail. If you tell no one, you have no one to betray you.

Stick with me, I've taken you to the beach but we haven't gone surfing yet. Ha ha.

In telling you what is really going on, I am inviting you into a world of believe it or not. I could just be pulling your leg. I am, after all, a storyteller and this could just be another story. Just one more book of mischief written by a no-eared fool. But then you must ask yourself if the no-eared fool is telling lies *all* the time or just some of the time. And ask yourself how come none of these murders has ever been solved – and why is the storyteller so convinced that none of them ever will be?

Is the storyteller himself part of the original thinking behind the longest hit list in Australian criminal history? Good question. I'm glad you've asked. If so, is the storyteller a key player in the massive disinformation programme that smoke screens the men behind it all? Could the storyteller himself be one of the men who helped to draw up the original death list? Good questions, all.

Sure, many of those who have died in the last few years have been enemies of the storyteller. Alphonse Gangitano, Mark Moran and others have died the most horrible and bloody deaths. Sure, I will not shed crocodile tears or alligator shoes for any of them. Sure, their deaths have resulted in renewed interests in my books, CDs, films and assorted arms of Chopper Inc, but don't think for a moment that I would assist in letting people leave this mortal place simply for profit and fun. Who do you think I am, some sort of psychopath?

No, no and no. Such a thought would simply be too fantastic to believe. Your legs are being pulled by the old leg-puller. And remember, when I pull a leg, sometimes they just come off in my hands. At least, the toes do.

You're so convinced I'm telling you a lie that you can't wait to get to the next page. I'm either one of the best liars in Australia or one of the best storytellers. You be the judge – as long as you don't sit in the Supreme Court.

Let's go back to 1991 ... three very old and close friends are sitting at a table in a back-street hotel in Collingwood. Three very hated and feared men, they are – outcasts not just from normal everyday society but also from a criminal world that neither wants nor trusts them.

Each of the three draws up his own personal hit list of 20 names. One man is to oversee the actual killings, the second to handle the funding and the third to control the disinformation that would smother the biggest death list ever put together in Australian criminal history. Sixty names.

The three men agree it would take years to complete the plan. There could not be wholesale slaughter or even the dimmest police and criminals would be able to see the three as the common denominator. It was to be done so slowly that the police who began looking at the first murders would be retired before the list was complete. No one would see the connection. You cannot follow the trail if it has grown over.

Revenge is a dish best eaten cold – and these three were nothing if not patient. They were prepared to let revenge freeze and thaw out before they were ready to act.

The team knew they would have to use other men to help, and, if necessary, kill them to ensure they remained silent. Dead men tell no tales.

They knew it could take 15 to 20 years. Some would die from natural causes, others would die at the hands of other enemies, but the list would grow and overflow, and end up being 80 or even 100. To win a war you can't have a time limit and you have to kill everybody and, naturally, over a 15- to 20-year period you find yourself planning the murders of men you hadn't known when the list was drawn up.

As I write this, the list is 15 down with seven helpers put off as a side issue in the name of silence. By the time I've finished writing this book there will have been 20 men crossed off the original list of 60, with maybe four to six more helpers having to go with them.

Then there will be a list of 40. Not too many really – you could put them all on one bus. Sixty sounds a bit hard to believe, but, when you read this and learn that there are only 40 more to go, it's not such a fantastic tale to believe, after all.

I mean, some mental retard in Tasmania killed nearly 40 innocent people in one afternoon at Port Arthur in 1996, so 40 more murders in Australia over 10 years isn't such a way-out thing. One difference being that the Port Arthur victims were decent citizens who didn't deserve to die, whereas the ones on the Collingwood list all have it coming.

The media will gobble it up as an underworld war. They will never know it is an extermination programme. With any luck, some of those on the list will blame others on the list for some of the deaths and start to kill each other.

It has happened at least twice in the last few years, and it saves us the effort if they do it to themselves.

When it's all over, the same three original thinkers will meet at the same pub in Collingwood and raise glasses of Irish whiskey and just nod. There will be nothing that will need to be said. That is if they haven't turned the old pub into a poker-machine dump or a coffee shop for trendies.

If they can put a man on the moon, you can kill him when he comes back to earth and then you can say, 'Shit, I just shot the man on the moon.' You might get put in a mental hospital but no one will ever believe you enough to send you to jail. That is the beauty of a death list so large. Who is ever going to believe it?

So there it is, the blueprint for a 20-year gang war hidden by a sea of bullshit, put together by the greatest criminal psychologist in the game, funded by cocaine dollars and heroin money handed over willingly by the new style of young Turks waiting to take over a criminal world and drug empire still ruled by men from the 1970s. Oh, I've forgotten the methamphetamine money.

The young drug dealers knew that if the dinosaurs of the criminal world fought then the ants might rule. But they didn't for a moment know the size of the plans.

The three original thinkers didn't take a penny of this cash. Every cent was spent on outside help, arms, ammo, travel, accommodation, logistic support, intelligence and counter intelligence. Spies and networks of spies, all working for controllers on a need-to-know basis within the various enemy camps. It is the greatest military criminal operation ever launched in Australian criminal history.

Why, you ask? To which the answer is: For the best reason of all … Why not?

If you sit by a river for long enough, you will see the bodies of all your enemies float by. I said that years ago. I forgot to mention that they will float past a damn sight quicker if you have a couple of mates upstream pushing the bastards in for you.

Eventually the bodies float down to the sea ... and the surf.

So, now, dear reader, we have our boards and we are about to enter water, and if you can't swim, don't worry. Uncle Chopper will reach out a hand and pull you back up. Would I tell a lie? Ha ha.

CHAPTER 2

OF MICE AND MEN (OR RATS AND REPORTERS)

what they lacked in honesty they
make up for in insincerity.

PLANS, like all plans of mice and men, can go wrong. One of the three original thinkers, the man given the job of providing a smother of disinformation and providing psychological tactics and strategy, got himself locked up over yet another shooting charge in 1992, so a replacement was invited to sit at the table.

The list of 20 names provided by the man now in jail was quietly replaced with a new list, which was put up by the new man. After all, fair is fair.

The new man, being an Italian criminal, had his own personal agenda and at least four of the names on his list matched the list of the third original thinker, now in prison. So we have the third original thinker in prison in 1992 saying *Via Con Dios, Amigos* to his two old friends and the new man, who was also an old friend. He was not plucked out of the personal columns in the paper. Whatever role he could play from behind bars regarding psychological, tactical and strategic help and advice he would give. It would be invaluable, as sometimes you can see better from a distance, even if there are bars in the way. I did some of my best planning while inside and I could see the mistakes that others were about to make.

However, his ability to provide the massive smother of disinformation via his police and media contacts had been cut to shreds. You can hardly call a press conference from H Division, although I did come close.

A new tactic of 'Chinese whispers', starting with one small truth along with one small lie into the ear of one small policeman and one or two crime reporters, had begun.

Being able to predict the deaths of underworld personalities shortly before their demise was a massive help in providing very believable disinformation. The crime reporters would believe everything you said if you gave them a tip on a murder about to happen. In the end, you could guide them where you wanted them (which was usually up their own bottoms).

You would talk to them. They would buy you a beer and a bad Irish feed cooked by a Chinaman from Footscray. Then they would bump up their expense accounts to make a profit. I have found that what they lack in honesty they make up for in insincerity. And, as the great Groucho Marx should have said, if you can do that you've got it made.

I mean, if you can predict a man's death a month before it happens then who will call into question the rest of your story? You then give former policemen and rival newspaper and TV reporters the same story knowing that they will then spread it for you.

You can turn a lie into the truth within a month. Police investigations are launched on the basis of one body and one lie. They then proceed to go no place. Into the valley of the blind and in any war it is always good to pop off a few non-event bastards who have nothing to do with anything other than the fact that they knew a few of the real targets.

It is a totally one-sided war, but it must appear to look like a gang war. In a gang war, both sides know who they are up against, but, in this war, only one side is getting hit by an enemy they cannot see and do not know.

It creates paranoia and, in some cases, friends turn on friends and kill each other. Once that starts to happen within the criminal world, your enemy will actually begin to kill himself for you. It could be suggested that the death of Mark Anthony Moran in June 2000 was clear evidence that the psychology of fear and paranoia had forced the enemy to proceed to kill themselves the way that a wild animal caught in a trap chews off its own leg to escape, only to bleed to death later on. What has been set in place cannot be undone.

Forty more to go.

Whether they do it to themselves, which could be the case in some areas, or whether the men who drew up the original list do it, for them nothing can stop it now.

It's like Dr Frankenstein's monster: once something is created, it is very hard to control it. The whole thing can take on a life of its own, leaving the original thinkers to sit and wonder about it all. Wonder or marvel at the monster they created, but, like Dr Frankenstein, the creators must be aware that the monster can turn on them at any time.

So the best idea is to quietly withdraw, watch and wait and simply allow the game to continue, directing play from time to time with a good hit or two and a few good lies just to keep the players interested.

Fantastic, isn't it? Quite simply outrageous and truly unbelievable. But where are the revenge killings, where are the arrests and convictions? There are none. War, what war?

The police and the media all sense they are watching the biggest gang war in Australian criminal history but they can't quite understand the logic of it. And, for the police and the media, if it doesn't make sense, they simply can't accept it. They look at each death in isolation or as a small group — a spate of murders over months or a couple of years. No one looks at all of them. They can't see the big picture, but only because no one looks.

When the three original thinkers all got together, none of it was meant to make any sense — after all, when you allow your enemy to know what is happening you also allow your enemy to counter-attack.

The three men with a small crew of helpers can't stand in the cold light of day and fight 30 men and expect to win. It has to be a war of shadows and smoke fought in the valley of total bullshit and darkness.

I must also add that, by the time this book comes out, the three young hit men, codenamed the Beach Boys, will almost certainly be very much dead. However, the catchphrase 'Let's Go Surfing' will be very much alive. Killing the killers is a key part of overall protection, although of course you don't tell the youngsters at the time. Too much information tends to destroy their enthusiasm for the task at hand.

You must remember that the three original thinkers spent their criminal lives in a never-ending state of blood war, and blood war is the only reason they ever got involved in crime in the first place. Money and conventional power had nothing to do with it.

The original thinkers took criminal violence to an almost Zen level. They are the river, therefore, they and only they will control which way the river flows.

For the original thinkers, it is a game of chess and they are the masters. They will either win the game or destroy the whole criminal structure as it stands. It is as simple as that. Either way they win.

You can believe this or disregard it as nonsense. I personally don't give a shit. I'm Mark 'Chopper' Read. I've written nine bestsellers and had a movie made about my life. Do you really think I give a shit who believes me or not? If you don't, you can always buy a newspaper and read how the media know all and claim that police know who did this, that and the other and are hoping for an early arrest. And they reckon *I'm* the one who's pulling people's legs.

We have now jumped on our surfboards and are heading out to meet our first big wave. Don't get seasick just yet.

Sometimes a story doesn't start at the start or finish at the end. I will simply toss the name of Liu Szu-Po into the pot and say no more. If war funding has to be provided and the Asians and their various crews are not part of any criminal culture, other than their own, the total destruction of the established order can only benefit their own ends.

I will repeat that name for the doubters reading this: Liu Szu-Po, a gentleman from Thailand. One of the original thinkers in charge of funding visited Thailand. Let's put it this way, I'm not the only man in the world with no ears and the fact that the chap in charge of funding also had no ears impressed Mr Liu Szu-Po enough to follow his way of thinking.

Any team of men who could carry out such savagery upon their own persons for reasons known only to themselves were the men to financially support in any conflict. Mr Liu Szu-Po is an international criminal thinker and is willing to fund criminal wars in cities all over the world between the various local factions if it means his own international network can slide into the play like a black snake on a dark night.

The original thinkers simply want to rid themselves of enemies made over decades, not to mention the relatives and friends and hangers-on of those enemies.

If it takes 15 to 20 years, it doesn't matter. The original thinkers will be in their sixties and by then an Asian wave will dominate a vast section of the international crime scene anyway.

Why not silently team up with the Triads? They at least have a sense of honour and the rare ability to keep their word along with their silence. So while we start to surf, let us remember the name *Liu Szu-Po*, and on that topic I think I've said quite enough. He may not be able to surf but he surely can hire the boards.

Let us now turn to probably the most two-bob nothing murder in Melbourne in recent times, the shooting of Richard Victor Mladenich at St Kilda's Esquire Motel in May 2000.

This was a straight Beach Boys hit. However, within moments, disinformation was put about that Mladenich was shot in error – in the wrong place at the wrong time.

His life as a standover man was nickel and dime stuff with street-level junkies and whores. He couldn't fight to save himself yet he had built up a violent and crazy reputation. In fact, he was a big heap of shit with the heart of a split pea – a homosexual rapist in prison who found himself on the wrong side of the Romanians. It is not a good place to be. His name wasn't even on the list. In fact, it was a case of someone not having a lot to do on the night in question, so they decided: 'Let's go and shoot him anyway.'

His death was a (very) red herring tossed into the pot to further bewilder and spin-doctor the minds of the already paranoid. Again, I don't feel the death of such a wombat should warrant too much writing time.

It was rumoured that I once put the blade of a garden spade through the right side of his skull, nearly killing him in H Division at Pentridge in 1989, but Richard stuck staunch and told the police nothing.

The two prison officers who witnessed it told the police nothing either. That's how H Division ran back then. Ah, the good old days.

The murder of Mad Charlie was for me a great personal sadness. I even named my son after him. He was, in spite of fallouts from the past, an old and dear friend.

A cunning campaign of disinformation was set in place to smother details of his death – details such as who might have done it, for instance. And why. All the wider world knows is that Charlie copped it in the front yard of his home in South Caulfield in November 1998, and that a .38 calibre weapon was involved. Apart from knowing that Charlie didn't die in his sleep of old age, the police seem to have no idea what really happened. Either that, or they're not that interested.

His name was never on the original list. However, his friendship with the three original thinkers meant that Charlie was starting to figure certain things out.

Now Charlie was mad, but he was also smart. For the original thinkers, the worry was that Charlie would put it all together and tell someone. He had some friends in the police force and the thinkers couldn't take the risk that he would get chatty.

Charlie was killed by a friend, a man who didn't want to kill him but could see no other way out of this particular problem.

Charlie had always said, 'When my time comes, let it not be at the hands of a laughing enemy but at the hands of a crying friend.' He got his wish. I can tell Charlie that the tears over what had to be done were flowing before his death and are still flowing. The same disinformation programme was brought into play. No more need be said on that topic.

Via Con Dios, Amigo
'Rest In Peace'
Charlie Hegyalji
23/11/98
'May God go with you'

The Beach Boys acted as logistic support on that hit, but a killing of such personal importance, not to mention sentiment, had to be carried out by a friend, not an enemy.

I had intended to name this book 'Surf's Up' or 'Let's Go Surfing' but the Beach Boys crew are a team that I'm sure will be dead by the time this book comes out and, therefore, it would be in poor taste. They were to be killed by the men who created them or they may even be simply added to the overall psychology of fear when their bodies are found.

If you give dogs the taste of blood you might have to kill them before they turn on you. So I've decided to call this part of the book 'Psychology of Fear', as basically the whole insane campaign relies heavily on this very psychology and the fact that the ordinary man will dismiss this story as the work of a mad man, whose whole life and the stories he tells have all been quite unbelievable.

That is my defence. I can write it all down in the comic knowledge that none of you will believe a word I'm writing. The only safe way to tell the truth is when you know people are convinced you're lying. Like when I told the police I killed Sammy the Turk, they just didn't believe me. Sammy did. But, sadly, he was in no condition to corroborate my story.

It was the confession and the story that went with it and the fact that the police did not act on a confession that ultimately helped the jury come to the wise decision that I was not guilty of murder.

But then, what would I know; after all, I am the greatest liar on earth. Would I tell anyone the truth?

So a wall of disbelief protects this whole story. Don't you think these tactics have ever been used before?

Hitler once said, 'The greater the lie, the more people will believe it.' Do you think that the truth is a weapon ever used in war?

John F. Kennedy. Martin Luther King. Do you really believe that disinformation wasn't the greatest weapon used before and after their deaths? The list goes on and on.

Just read history – military history, political history, any sort of history.

The people either don't want to, or simply will not, believe the truth, so a lie must be created for them. When a writer writes about lies, how can he ever be sued or charged for telling the truth?

I feel I sit here writing this with a certain legal safety. I will repeat, you can either believe it or not, I will not confirm nor will I deny. You be the jury.

The Beach Boys' first real hit wasn't about California girls or little red

Corvettes. It was a Chinese gentleman who came visiting Australia and didn't survive the trip. The less said about that the better, as even words smothered under the shadow of fiction from the pen of a self-confessed storyteller, leg puller and yarn spinner might be taken entirely the wrong way.

Their second job, acting as a back-up crew providing logistic support, was the Gangitano hit in January 1998. They were there to make sure the first crew went in and did the job.

Gangitano's name was placed on the list by the Italian who replaced the third original thinker and as a personal favour to the same man. To have Alphonse Gangitano's own friends carry out most of the mission by setting him up took nearly three years of disinformation and inside spy work to convince the men closest to Alphonse that he had been acting as a Federal and NCA and DEA informer for the six years prior to his death. It was probably the greatest chess game played by the original thinkers, although by no means the only one.

At first, his friends would not believe the stories that he was an informer, but after the seed was sown the poisonous plant was always going to grow in the minds of the paranoid.

For the sake of this story I will call the Italian, who joined the original thinkers, 'the Pizza Man'. Not very inventive, I know, but it will have to do.

Their third main hit was in 1999. The target was Dimitrious Bellas, nicknamed 'Jimmy the Greek'. The Pizza Man himself, along with one of the original thinkers, Mr Blue Eyes, aided by the three Beach Boys, went on to do Vince Mannella in January 1999, and his brother Gerry or Gerardo Mannella in October 1999.

The Beach Boys helped a Romanian crew kill Danny Boy Mendoza and seven other Romanians who remain on the missing list to date. Some of them were illegal immigrants and so there were no records of them being here in the first place. They could hardly be missed. Those who knew they were on the missing list were too frightened to say anything. There were wives who would never mention that their husbands had disappeared. Many knew the truth but would never tell any authorities.

All together, the Beach Boys crew, Mr Blue Eyes and the Pizza

Man have carried out approximately 15 murders since 1997 and that does not include the deaths of helpers brought in to dig graves, mix acid, drive trucks and getaway cars and provide safe-house locations.

They even killed one helper for arriving 30 minutes late to a meeting and using a taxi to get to the motel where the Pizza Man was staying. He was told to travel by train and then walk, and to be on time.

You can't run a top hit team with your staff not showing up for work or showing up late and not following orders.

To top it off, he didn't have the money to pay the taxi, which brought the driver to the motel front desk. The whole operation had to be cancelled – all because of a sloppy employee.

You might read this and question why I'm dancing over the deaths of targets in such a light-hearted manner and not spending pages and pages on each one, filling you with boring detail regarding what a dark night it was and how the moonlight shone on the gun barrel. What I can say is that the video camera was turned off but not the automatic garden sprinkler system, meaning everyone arrived back wringing wet.

Yet, by the time the police arrived, someone had turned off the sprinkler. No, I won't go into detail, or I'd have to say that Mad Charlie always kept his front doorway light on so his front door and garden area was well lit when he arrived home. But, the funny thing was that on the night he died the light was off. This great piece of good luck helped hide the killer, who was under the front hedge. It was a tight fit but Charlie's old friend was not a heavy fellow so he could slip in there quite comfortably to wait to deliver the death sentence to a mate.

I will say that in some cases even the best hit crew cannot carry out their work without a little inside help.

Let me put this argument to you. If a woman is told that either her husband is to die or her children, one or the other, which one would she pick? This is not what happened with Mad Charlie but it could have been used in other cases. There is always a way to get someone to help you. You just have to find the way in each case. In Charlie's case, there were friends and also people who *pretended* to be his friends. The underworld is full of people who pretend to be your friends and others who pretend to be your enemies.

I do not intend to waste my time or yours writing about the life and times and deaths of any particular individual. This book is meant to be a psychological, tactical and strategic overall view of certain deaths.

Take Mark Moran ... please. Sorry, couldn't resist the old Henny Youngman gag. But seriously, to get Moran killed, a person close to him, a very powerful friend and business partner, had to be totally convinced that he was guilty of a grievous wrongdoing.

To convince an already paranoid man that he has been betrayed by a close friend isn't as hard as it sounds, especially when the powerful criminal in question is married to a slut former junkie whore who has never told the truth in her life.

The very fact that she screamed her innocence while being bashed only proved her supposed guilt. Then, when she screamed in rage, 'Yeah, I fucked him and I loved it. Why wouldn't I?' the fact that Moran wouldn't touch the ugly old slag with a 40-foot pole was beside the point.

If either of the Morans was screwing the wife, then they might have been behind a police raid that cost this particular gangster and his team millions in lost goods and legal fees. All of this, of course, was disinformation put out by Mr Blue Eyes and the Pizza Man via the Chinese, a good 12 months before Moran's death.

The gangster in question did big business with the Chinese and Vietnamese. Why would they lie? They were making good money together. Well, they weren't lying – they were simply repeating what they had been told by an Italian visiting Thailand on holiday.

The disinformation about Moran originated in Thailand but was set in place in Melbourne. You see how a Chinese whisper campaign works. Even if it's not believed.

The named person has to be killed because there is simply too much at stake to risk. After all, these men aren't running a charity and you can forget all the loving death notices in the newspaper. There were pages of death notices for Mark Moran and Alphonse Gangitano. Many of the mourners were sincere but there were as many who were happy to see them dead.

Tears mean nothing when they are insincere. Even real tears can conceal a murderer. The deep thinkers who put Mad Charlie off still miss him greatly, but sometimes things have to be done. The sentimental gangster will die or spend his life in jail. Only the cool heads and the cold-hearted survive.

None of these men really trusts each other. The game is so easy it is almost child psychology. Add the use of cocaine to this mix and the psychology of fear, using death, paranoia and disinformation, is damn near foolproof.

The enemy simply cannot afford not to take action – they have too much to lose. Fortunes, friends and family. The more you have, the more frightened you become of losing. There is an old saying that property makes cowards of us all. It's true, even in the criminal world. The up-and-coming gangster is the most dangerous because he has nothing to lose. Once he has made a mark, settled down with a family and begun raking in the cash, he is terrified. Frightened someone will target him, take his spot, take his money, tell the cops and ruin his party. Most of the time he is right.

In that world, you can't afford to let a man live just because he might be a good bloke and might not be an informer. Might not means that he also might be. Only death will make sure he isn't. Simple as that. You are the weakest link – bang! It takes the guess out of the guessing game.

We are riding the surf now, dear reader. Are you standing up yet, or have you lost your balance and fallen in? Be careful, the sharks are everywhere, and not just in the water.

It is also true that most of the top drug criminals in Melbourne and Sydney have some form of relationship with some police. So it is not hard to convince a paranoid drug boss that so-and-so is an informer because he thinks to himself, Well, *I've* got my police that I talk to, why should he be the odd man out?

The fire is already set, you just have to find the right match. It's simply a matter of knowing thy enemy and know him very well. Are you seeing now how the original list of 60 men to be killed over a 15- to 20-year period wasn't really so far-fetched at all?

Think of the murders that remain unsolved. Freddie the Frog lost half his head in the docks back in the 1950s. His mate, Big Normie, fell out of the sky not long after. The Ferret went swimming in his

Valiant. It wasn't roadworthy, or seaworthy. Painters and Dockers painted themselves into dark corners, drug dealers went on missing lists and crooks retired into shallow graves. The police didn't try too hard. Many thought the crims got their right whack. The coppers, meanwhile, were trying to solve murders of innocent people. When they deal with crims who either won't talk or talk bullshit, they lose interest pretty quickly. In fact, in the light of the psychology used, I think 60 was quite modest.

Let us now return to 12 November 1979, and a man by the name of Raymond Patrick Chuck, head of the crew that carried out the Great Bookie Robbery on the Victorian Club in Queen Street on 26 April 1976. The papers said it was believed between $1 and $12 million was taken. I have always believed it was $6 million, but some very good judges, who know how much bookies were holding and how much they owed, calculate that it was a bit less than that. In any case, it was still plenty of money for those days, so who's counting?

Ray Chuck was shot dead as he was escorted through the Melbourne Magistrates' Court. The rumours put about were that the late criminal gang leader and standover merchant Brian Kane pulled the trigger as a payback for the death of his brother, Leslie Herbert Kane.

Whispers were then heard that professional hit man Christopher Dale Flannery, nicknamed 'Rent-A-Kill', did the job, setting in place probably the greatest disinformation campaign ever conceived. If Ray Chuck was killed by Flannery then the answer to who killed Flannery is too fucking easy.

Who was Ray Chuck's best friend in the world? I won't name him, as he is still alive and remains one of the best crooks in Australia. He isn't a bad bloke at all and certainly doesn't deserve to do a life sentence over a maggot like Flannery.

To add punch to the party you had all these razzle-dazzle Sydney gangsters either bragging that they shot Flannery or that they knew who did. So the disinformation campaign put in place to protect the true identity of the man who did kill Flannery wasn't hard, but it was massive, and went on for years.

It's hard to come back and say, 'Oh, by the way, to prove my point on the psychology of criminal gang warfare, fear and the sheer power of disinformation, I'd now like to confess that I invented 90 per cent of the crap people now believe to be fact surrounding the Flannery case.' That would be stupid, wouldn't it?

Now, it is true that the team carrying out the inquest into the death of sad old Chris did come down to Risdon Prison in sleepy Tassie to have a chat. They asked me many questions. I can understand why they would want my views on such a serious matter. After all, with all due modesty, I do possess the greatest criminal mind of any (living) underworld identity. Which proves mainly that there aren't that many heavy thinkers in criminal ranks.

Anyway, so they rocked down for a chat. I spoke for a great deal of time. They listened, took more notes and nodded gravely. I nodded gravely. They asked more questions and took more notes. Each one of them got more than a grand a day for asking questions. I got bugger all for answering them. They went back to their five-star hotels to mull over what I had said with the help of a cheeky Pinot and a local lobster. I had rissoles for tea washed down with some prison hooch. You work it out.

They seemed happy. I was happy. Did I feed them some disinformation? Perish the thought. As a law-abiding citizen – not – I did my best to help, but no one (including me) has done a day's jail over Chris, who, rumour suggests, may have given a white pointer shocking heartburn.

The beauty of being a known killer and an alleged author is that you can have an opinion on any murder and people don't know if it is a theory based on experience or the facts based on inside knowledge. Sometimes I don't know myself. I prefer not to. It's less complicated.

Take poor Alphonse. Some pretty young television thing wanted me to debate him when I got out of jail. I told the little vixen that it was not to be unless it was done through a Ouija board, as Al was about to cop a couple of lead injections in his cranium.

As suspected, Alphonse ran out of breath rather suddenly just a few weeks later. Was that inside knowledge or just a lucky guess? Any fool could see that Alphonse was running red hot and couldn't be allowed to keep going. But then again, I'm no fool.

Whether I had inside knowledge or just suspected what was going to happen doesn't matter. He is dead and I am not. I can't be blamed as I was inside Risdon, well out of harm's way.

The same applies to the murder, still unsolved, of Tony Franzone, shot six times in May 1992. His death is so long ago and so unsolved it has been forgotten. Although shrouded in the mist of time and disinformation, it is an important key to unlocking the coffin that Alphonse Gangitano finally went into.

Underworld hits are never solved unless, of course, your name is Billy 'The Texan' Longley and your hit squad is made up of mental retards with mouths like running taps.

But, in general, a professional hit will go unsolved forever, shrouded in a sea of bullshit, created by men who know psychology. What the police and media are willing to believe. The police and media are pretty black and white thinkers, so any red herring tossed their way must be big enough to catch and small enough to eat. Disinformation within the criminal world must be the size of a fucking battleship as paranoid people eat, drink, live and sleep on a never-ending diet of conspiracy theories. All you have to do is create a story that links their name into it all and they will believe anything.

They get on the phone to their own police and media contacts and within two days, my police and media contacts are telling me of a whole new line of investigation. I back down and reply, 'Gee, I was sure my information was correct.' They put the phone down, smugly thinking that fucking Read isn't the fucking know-it-all he thinks he is. I put the phone down and simply smile. Gotcha! Ha, ha, ha!

Media and police rely on information received. All you have to do is create the information they receive, then control it and never rely on one story. Always give them several sources, then allow them to select the most tasty piece of rubbish from the menu. Never force feed them; allow them the pleasure of a la carte. If they pick their own, they will believe it more.

I know of several investigations, still unsolved, where police scientific investigators mistook a gunshot wound from a .22-calibre magnum handgun for that of a 38-calibre.

The slug passed straight through the body and was never found, so the whole homicide squad is busy, busy, busy sorting out the disinformation on murders they will never solve, beginning with scientific evidence, sending the investigators in search of the wrong weapon. How do I know that? Maybe I made it up, or maybe I know the killer. Maybe I know the killer very well.

I won't start on police scientific investigators. Remember the Azaria Chamberlain case. Blood spots, which turned out to be paint spots when they entered the courtroom. It's a nice trip up the yellow brick road.

Scientific evidence doesn't have to be 100 per cent spot on any more. The introduction of DNA evidence means that all that is needed now is to be pretty close, not 100 per cent. But a fair chance and that's that, you're guilty. Add that crap to police evidence based on several years of disinformation along with police ballistic experts who can't tell a .22-calibre magnum head wound from the head wound of a .38. I can think of several fellows, although very guilty of a hundred other unsolved crimes, who didn't do the ones they are in prison for. Quite comic really, in a poetic-justice sort of way. Life all seems to equal itself out in the end. Just ask Alphonse. His equalled itself out a little earlier than he'd hoped. Never mind, if he believed in reincarnation, perhaps he'll get a longer tour of duty next time.

But I'm getting off the track.

Remember Victor Frederick Allard, a former painter and docker turned drug dealer? He was shot to death in February 1979, in Fitzroy Street, St Kilda. And Michael Ebert, who was shot to death on 17 April 1980, outside a brothel in Rathdowne Street, Carlton? Both unsolved. Police and media all think they know the answer, but if they know so fucking much then how come no arrests or convictions?

Did Shane Goodfellow really die of a drug overdose in 1992 or was it a hotshot murder? The same with Tony MacNamara – but, again, I digress. I tend to do this. The reader must forgive me.

Trying to write a book while stopping my 10-month-old baby son, Charlie, from smashing the TV remote control over the cat's head tends to distract one's Thomas the Tank Engine of thought. Charlie is, as I said, 10 months old at the time of writing and two stone in weight, with four teeth already, and walking, albeit with help. He enjoys chewing the skin off raw potatoes. As you do.

Anyway, I have to put the pen down to change Charlie's nappy.

From murder to nappies, life has indeed taken me on some strange twists and turns. Although, looking at it, I think he has committed GBH of the bottom. As often happens, I sit down to write thinking that I'm heading in a certain direction, only to find I have begun a literary U-turn. This, I guess, is my style. It was the same when I was full-time in the underworld. I might pop around to someone's place for a drink, then decide to shoot them in the guts or just burn their house down. Poor old Nick the Greek still whinges about that. He should remember that, without me, he would have been just another no-name drug dealer. With my help, free of charge, he ended up in the *Chopper* movie and is world famous. God help us all.

The fact that no one knew whether I was coming around for a drink (as in Victoria Bitter) or coming around for a 'drink' (as in a sling) always added a tingle to your underworld social event. Will I have a Harvey Wallbanger, or just grab Harvey and bang him into the wall? These were the sorts of questions which kept everyone interested in the social whirl.

There is much that I miss about the old days. The torture, the blood, the look in a drug dealer's eyes over those few hours it takes them to remember where the stash is. The look of fear as they know there will be pain; the look of anger as they know they will lose their cash; the look of hope when they think that will be enough; the look of resignation as they hop in the boot and the look for their mother when they see the lime and the spade.

You could write a book about it, except I already have.

> 'Mentally speaking, it's pretty hard to pull your socks up when you're only wearing fucking thongs.'
>
> FRANKIE WAGHORN, H DIVISION LEGEND AND THE HARDEST PUNCHER
> IN THE UNDERWORLD

I'm not the only one to use the psychology of fear or to weave a web of disinformation to conceal the truth.

Take the case of Santo Ippolito in December 1991. Santo was bashed to death in his home in Springvale. Case unsolved. Disinformation within underworld circles claimed that a member of my crew hired through me was paid to do it. I've never heard of the bloke in my life.

And, if I did, I wouldn't tell you. I didn't get all this way to lag myself back into jail. Twenty-four years is enough for anyone.

Take the case of Vietnamese drug dealer Quock Cuong Dwong, killed on 30 January 1992. There was a story put about it was a torture job again. Again, there were baseless rumours that members of my old crew were close to the scene. There was even one yarn that had me actually involved. Again, never heard of the bloke. I am offended by these slanders against me.

But the best was when the Italians killed Rocco Medici and his brother Giuseppe Furina and dumped them in the Murrumbidgee River after cutting their ears off. I'm unsure of the date, but it was back in the eighties and it may have been 5 May 1984, at a spooky guess.

It was during the height of the Pentridge Overcoat Gang war and a membership drive of the Van Gogh club, which is far more exclusive than the Melbourne club. Members of my crew, on the outside, were rumoured to have been paid by the Italians to carry out the murders, and the ears was a comic touch. A sort of Van Gogh signature.

In all of the history of the Italian criminal culture, ear cutting has never been a part of the play. That bit of disinformation lasted about two days until a few were told that the next lot of ears to come off would be their own. End of disinformation programme, but they are still unsolved murders.

And, now, if I may quote myself from an earlier work regarding these matters: 'If you have a dead body in the bottom of your swimming pool and the police are on their way over to interview you about a missing wristwatch, then the only thing you can do is toss dirt into the pool and muddy the water. What people can't see, they won't worry about. The police may remark on your dirty swimming pool but, for the time being, that's it until the next move, which is hopefully out of the fucking swimming pool.'

To which I would add a thought from Sherlock Holmes: 'Ninety per cent of all criminal cases solved are the direct result of information received. The remaining 10 per cent belong to the investigating criminal detective and 9 per cent of those cases are bungled by forensic fools. The impossible 1 per cent are totally unsolvable. The per cent remaining is then handed to us, my dear Watson.'

CHAPTER 3

MYTHS AND LEGENDS

sometimes real bullets
are needed.

MANY years ago, around 1969, in the midst of street fights and teenage-gang trouble in Thomastown, I had taken to covert action against my enemy. Rocks through windows at night. A petrol can and a box of matches left at a front doorstep. A .22-calibre slug from a bolt-action rifle through the front door at night. Death-threat phone calls. Turning their power off at night. Home-made fire bombs tossed at front doors. In several cases, I burned down their outside Thunderbox dunny toilets. I'd slash the tyres on the family car. Put bricks through the windscreen. In several cases, I'd poison the family dog.

Generally, I was a 15-year-old arsehole, and to top it off I started to spread rumours that these covert activities were being carried out by three criminal brothers, Nick, Paul and Rocco Shachini. The rumours spread over the years. I would hear that this or that unsolved murder or shooting was carried out by the brothers.

When I first met Mad Charlie, he had heard the feared reputation of the shadowy brothers and was impressed that I knew them. Alphonse Gangitano claimed to actually know the fabulous Shachini brothers.

Personally, I stopped telling wild Shachini brother stories in about 1975, but it was too late – the imaginary Shachinis had taken on a life all of their own in the form of a Sicilian Mafia family from Thomastown who secretly controlled Italian criminal concerns throughout the northern suburbs in the eighties.

I was often asked if I knew them or had heard of them, by men claiming to know them and to be criminally involved with them. I then would reply that, like others, I'd heard of them but had never met them.

It had long been forgotten by the teenage kids of years ago that Chopper Read was the first one ever to mention the Shachini brothers.

In 1987, an old Italian man who I will call Poppa Tony told me that the former NSW vice king Maltese Joe Borg was blown to death in his car in 1969 on the orders of the Shachini brothers. Poppa Tony wasn't lying – he was repeating a story he believed to be true.

The Shachini brothers were also rumoured to have disposed of the mortal remains of anti-drug campaigner Donald Mackay. And they were rumoured to be the private hit squad behind the international drug king Howard Marks. The name of the three brothers has now run its natural course and they are only spoken of in whispers by old men and men who are desperate to find the answer to an unsolvable riddle.

But, for a time, this invented myth played a large role in my own disinformation campaigns and helped to create my own personal method of tactical and strategic gang warfare, which I would later call my 'psychology of fear' theory. I would refine it over the years but what I learned when I was 15 was to become the biggest plank of my methods – and many a crook would be forced to walk it before I was done.

It wasn't courage or bravery that made me disregard most of what I heard from criminals, media and police regarding rumoured death contracts on my own life. Fact was, various times I was told the contracts had been ordered by the great Shachini brothers themselves. I mean, the whole criminal world was a mishmash of bullshit with a dead body or two tossed in the pot now and again to add weight to the raging river of lies. Was it any wonder that no one could stop me from laughing? I wasn't mad, I just knew the truth, a truth that no one would ever believe.

As a master of propaganda, I could pick a disinformation campaign from a distance. Don't kid a kidder and don't bullshit a killer. Most of these stories I knew were fairy-tales and those that weren't ... well, sometimes spin-doctors weren't enough. Sometimes, real bullets were needed.

Why is it so? Because some nitwit has put it in writing and told you it is so. Read the Bible, and then tell me that people can't be tricked by disinformation. People believe what they want to believe. In the criminal world, the only trick is to come up with disinformation that the crims, media and police can all agree on. That's why the poor old general public has done more bulk swallowing than Linda Lovelace. A book on *true* crime – I doubt that such a book has ever been written, in the history of man. The closest would be the most excellent *Underbelly* series which I keep on my bedside table for night-time reading.

We are now surfing in a sea of disinformation. It's night time and we can't see the sky or the beach. We are just surfing in the direction that the waves are taking us. We are all surfing on a lie. The only truth is, if we fall in, we die.

Are you beginning to understand the world I'm trying to take you to? What the media, police, writers and movie directors call the underworld. The logic is to ignore logic. You have to unlearn what you have been taught.

That is why people, including police, never truly understand the underworld. They think too much. They start by saying, 'If I was the crook, I would have done this.' They give most crooks too much credit for planning and logic. Dennis Allen shot a bloke for putting the wrong record on in his lounge room. Work that out – he would have been a shocking DJ.

We had a war in jail because I was alleged to have eaten too many sausages, a foul piece of slander indeed – although I must say they were yummy.

Nothing makes sense and, when you understand that, everything falls into place. There is no logic in shooting someone outside a crowded nightclub, cutting your ears off and baseball-batting various fat wombats in front of witnesses.

There is no master plan, just a sea of human filth trying to get to the surface for a breath of pure air. I have known of crims on their way to a million-dollar heroin deal who have shoplifted a coat on the way. If they had been caught, the deal would have gone sour. Why did they do it? Because they could.

End of story, or rather, just the beginning. Are you getting the picture? Do you want me to draw a map? You're in Northern Ireland and a man walks up to you in the dark and puts a loaded gun to your head. He pulls the hammer back and asks, 'What religion are you?' You have but a few seconds to reply or die, and the wrong reply will kill you. To reply and prevent the gunman from killing you, then to make him puzzle and think and look and ask questions, allowing you precious seconds to somersault the whole situation. It is the trick and the trick is disinformation.

How would you reply? I've spent most of my life, not only replying in the correct manner, but also walking away with the gunman's weapon and him convinced that he was lucky to get out of the situation with his life. That, my dear reader, is the psychology of fear. Master that and you can master the world. It is bluff, backed by a baby .410 shotgun and an army of psychopaths. The art is looking out of control when you are very much in control.

You're still surfing in the dark, aren't you? Let's hope that, when you get to the last page, you will see the sunlight. I will have to expose myself and, after nine bestsellers, three music CDs, a movie made about my life, a sunglasses contract and an international profile, it may be time to expose the real me.

Or not.

What do I care? I've won the game and telling you, even in a small way, how I did it will not be considered bragging, I would hope. A magician is not a liar or a conman. He has just made you believe that what you didn't see really did happen and what you really did see didn't happen at all. If he can make you laugh at the same time, you belong to him, for he has, for a moment, captured your imagination. I am the magician who doesn't pull a rabbit from his hat but a pistol from his underpants.

Many years ago, a very well-known radio type, later to become a TV personality, was debating the rape issue on talkback radio with a high-profile lady in the women's movement. She stopped him dead by saying, 'Well, it's a waste of my time debating this point with you. You have never been raped – I have.'

The next day, the radio personality shocked his listeners by breaking down and tearfully confessing that he had been the victim of sexual molestation as a child at the hands of his uncle. Game, set and match to him. He had not only won the debate but also gained the sympathy of a whole new audience.

The only evidence that what he said was true was his own word. But why would a man say such a thing if it weren't true? Why, indeed! Think of the psychological advantage. Another famous personality comes out and confesses to being homosexual, then writes a bestseller on the topic. The truth was he was really straight and just pretending to be gay.

How many famous American TV and movie personalities have broken down in tears on national television with stories like 'Daddy played with my rubber duckie in the bath when I was six and my mother held me at gunpoint while he did it'? There are too many to count.

It all comes back to what Hitler said about people always believing a really big lie. Chopper Read comes out and tells people he has murdered 19 people and, bang, he's a psycho killer overnight.

No one stops to say, hang on, hang on, let's have a look at this. Some half-retarded moll says she is the mother of Mick Jagger's love child and bingo! That's that. Elvis Presley isn't really dead. Adolf Hitler was seen sunning himself outside a cafe in Argentina in 1967. Lee Harvey Oswald really did shoot Kennedy.

Did they really put a man on the moon or was it a CIA/White House/Hollywood con trick to kid the world and the USSR that the Americans did it?

OK, OK, that's a bit far-fetched, although it wouldn't surprise me if Dave the Jew was the first man on the moon – or shot the bloke who was.

What I am getting at is we believe most of what we are told or what we read or see on the six o'clock news. It is human nature to want to believe what we are hearing and reading. If we do not believe what we are told, what have we got left? What fills the void?

We all know politicians are liars, yet we not only vote them into office, we also pay them a lot of money and we believe what they tell us while knowing all the time that most of them can't be trusted.

What does that tell us about human nature? For Christ's sake, I'm probably the greatest liar and disseminator of disinformation in Australian criminal history. Let's face it, I'm a raving bullshit artist but

I can make people laugh while telling them a lie, and, psychologically, if a person is laughing while listening to or reading a story, then he or she is subconsciously believing that story. You can't shoot me when you're laughing, but I am the master of the side-splitting joke. Literally.

Yes, I have shot a few and a few have died – big deal. But, in reality, Chopper Read was a less than average criminal who used greater than average violence for less than average money. But Chopper Read could spin a greater than above-average story and he could get people laughing. I'm a self-made man with an unmade face and an unfilled grave. It has now reached the stage that fact can no longer be separated from fiction.

That's what a true legend is. A legend is a myth. It is a lie welded together with the truth and used as a cosh to beat the unsuspecting around the head. I've done it and now I'm telling you; believe nothing except what you yourself believe to be true while all the time being aware that you could be wrong.

I will take a little mental rest now. My doctor warned me not to get into these spinouts as I start to waffle and I suspect I'm starting to rave a little. Then again, sometimes the truth of a situation can be clearly seen only after talking to a total mental case.

I must go and find one.

A mate of mine, Shane Farmer, a local nightclub owner, once said to me, 'Chopper, you have created a legend and built yourself into a national celebrity and now you want to come back and write a book and tell everyone it is all bullshit. Why?'

No, I don't, my point is that it *could* all be bullshit. For example, take Dave the Jew. Until I mentioned him in my first book, no one had ever heard of him. Now he is being blamed for unsolved murders all over Melbourne. They even questioned him over the death of Alphonse.

Yes, I know a bloke named Dave and, yes, he is a Jew, but I created his reputation and I created a legend.

Was it all fact or fantasy? Only *I* will ever know. Dave and me, that is. Now the legend of Dave the Jew, thanks to me, has taken on a life all of its own. This is my point, it's not hard to create a myth or a legend or give a totally unknown a feared reputation, then to step back and watch your own creation take on a life all of its own. Criminals are by nature all liars. Police run a close second and the media outdo the both of us, so how can the general public believe a single word?

That is what I'm trying to say. Who created Chopper Read? Well, first of all, I did it myself with some big help from the police. Then, of course, the media got in for its chop, if you know what I mean. Chopper Read's image is largely a media-created package. A virtual-reality, multi-media package with no ears and a heap of tattoos tied up in a bow.

But I wrapped the package for them, handed it to the police and together we handed it to the media. Dave the Jew – I could kill him off in the third page of my next book and the real Dave could scream to the wind. As far as the police, media and general public would be concerned, the Jew would be dead.

That's how easy it is to build a legend, then to kill one off. It's like writing characters in and out of television scripts, except that it's real life. I plant the seed, I can chop the tree. Within the criminal world, the lie is everything. The gun is only a tool used to support the lie – once you understand that, you begin to understand the insane psychology of it all.

Chopper Read is who and what you think he is because he told you he is. Others have confirmed my reality because I told them it was so. Maybe I don't exist at all. How many of you have seen me in the flesh? Only a few dozen people of the hundreds of thousands who have read the books and seen the movie.

They made the movie about my life based on what I wrote. OK, the movie is pretty well true – a few murders, a shooting or two and a bit of a huff and puff, but hardly the stuff legends are built on.

But if I can do it, what about the truth of other legends? What about reputations? Is it all just a lie? No, of course it isn't, but, for all that, in the criminal world the lie is vital. It is the glue that holds it all together.

The crims who have stolen this book will begin to understand but I suspect the rest of you will be struggling with it. Bear with me, it will all come together in the end.

People like things black and white. They don't like to be taken through the valley of the shadow of grey and no one likes to be told that what they believe isn't true or even isn't quite true. People want to believe in life after death. That's why the Bible is the best-selling book in the world.

No one really believes it, but with all their heart they want to believe it. So, too, with crime, the criminals, police, media and general public. They want to believe that a story, a legend, a reputation or a myth is true and so they dismiss anything other than what they want to believe. It is a mental, emotional and psychological weakness in all of us. I just know about it and can therefore use it against the rest. No one is immune.

Now I've given everyone a nice headache, let us move along.

After the 1987 Jika Jika fire in Pentridge Prison, in which five inmates died, the Russell Street bombing gang, along with myself and a handful of other maximum-security inmates, were moved back to the old H Division, my old home.

Believe this or not. I don't care. The police were spending a fortune on witness protection for the main crown witness, a former member of my old Overcoat Gang, a weasel we booted out for cowardice in the face of the enemy, Paul Kurt Hetzel. He has a full name change now and is living in a supposedly secret location interstate – so secret I could find him in the time it would take me to say Dave the Jew.

The police believed that the Russell Street bombers and their friends and contacts had the power to have Hetzel killed in 1988 – or was it 1989, I forget – but as their trial was under way I was approached by two members of the gang to see if I could arrange a handgun. Could I arrange a handgun? Could the Pope find some rosary beads?

Of course, I could arrange a handgun with a phone call. The code for handgun back then among my own contacts was Frankie. Could you get Frankie to meet so and so on Saturday morning etc.? I wasn't told why they wanted the handgun and ammo but you wouldn't need to be a big thinker to work it out. It would cost a thousand dollars.

They didn't have a thousand dollars, so no handgun. So let's look at that, shall we. The police were spending a million or more on protecting Paul Kurt Hetzel and his de facto along with other witnesses from a gang and their friends and criminal contacts, who, between the lot of them, couldn't come up with a thousand dollars.

For a grand, maybe the history of the bombing would have been rewritten, or maybe the prosecution would have been blown to the shithouse.

I've never mentioned this before as I didn't want to embarrass Craig Minogue, aka Fatty or Slim, who had done me a big favour in killing Alex Tsakmakis. But it was all years ago and, to prove my point, I will tell this story.

You see, as a direct result of disinformation and the psychology of fear, the Russell Street bombing gang were being treated like Mafia bosses in an Italian prison. It was widely believed they had vast criminal power and contacts.

However, in truth, they didn't have a popgun or a grand between the lot of them. Now the disinformation was being put about by the crown witnesses to bolster their own situation with the police. The police in turn handed the same fearful disinformation to the media. The psychology of criminal fear used by the bombing gang itself was in the form of the bombing attack on police headquarters in Russell Street.

Everyone believed these blokes were the Aussie version of the fucking IRA, but in reality the whole gang would have run a poor second to the Bananas in Pyjamas. You could have put the star witnesses in a motel room in St Kilda, with a neon sign out the front flashing the words 'Crown Witness Motel' and the Russell Street bombers would not have had the criminal clout to organise a rock-tossing contest through the motel windows.

That is the fact of the matter, but the fiction and the psychology of fear kept several teams of police busy 24 hours a day for several years, costing a fortune protecting witnesses from a phantom – a gang of wombats who couldn't organise a three-seated shithouse without getting one of the pans blocked up.

I won't make any friends by saying this, not that I ever had any friends to start with, just a couple of greedy publishers with a dodgy laptop and a lot of orthodontist bills. Fatty Minogue is a good bloke who did me a big favour when he opened up Alex's head but he is no Dr No, believe me.

You might be wondering how I can say that someone like Minogue is a good bloke. Here is a lesson in prison politics for the uninitiated. You don't make too many judgements about what people have done on the outside; it is how they behave on the inside that matters.

Sure, I might have put the occasional broom handle up the bottom of the (very) odd rapist if they deserved it. It was a hobby of mine, a little like stamp collecting. Of course, I did not like child molesters and such like, but it was not my job to be the judge of all the filth that floated into my division.

You make and then break alliances to keep control of the division. You are surrounded by some very seriously dangerous people (and that's just the prison warders) so you need soldiers to protect the general's back. Churchill had no time for Stalin, either, but was prepared to back him when Hitler invaded Russia. He said he would make a pact with the Devil if the Devil was prepared to have a sneaky go at Hitler. That's what jail is like. An enemy of your enemy is a friend. It's been true for thousands of years, and will be for thousands more.

Alex Tsakmakis was a millionaire and a killer. He chucked a professional runner named Bruce Walker in the bay in 1978. Walker was a good runner, but not much of a swimmer, which was no surprise given that he was trussed up in chicken wire at the time.

Tsakmakis then set fire to Barry Robert Quinn in Jika Jika in 1984. Quinn had baited him about his girlfriend, which was a dumb move. Alex squirted him with glue and then flicked matches at Barry. Whoosh! Barry was burned alive. Not a good way to go. And the scorched smell was around for days.

There was a death notice the next day that was supposed to come from Alex saying, 'Sorry, we always stuck together.' Call me a cynic but I reckon there was a touch of 'blue' humour in that one.

I stabbed Alex in the neck once, while he was reading the *Financial Review* in the exercise yard. He wasn't too tough when he was screaming around with blood pissing out where his collar used to be. He always was a pain in the n... Listen, for this price you can cop the odd bad pun.

After that, Alex and I became allies, even though he hated me. We had another dangerous opponent so we stuck together. Remember, the enemy of my enemy is my friend.

But, much later, after Minogue joined the division, I heard that Alex had put a $7,000 contract out on me. Now, that was a lot of money inside – for that sort of cash, I would nearly have done it myself.

I was saddened. Our alliance was over – although Alex didn't know it. He came to me with the plan to kill big Craig. He had a leather punch spike he wanted to drive into Craig's brain.

I warned Fatty Minogue about the attack. The big fella was to lose so much weight he was called Slim. Should have been called Jenny Craig Minogue.

When Alex went into the yard, Craig was waiting with a couple of gym weights in a pillow case. He wasn't looking for a workout. He swung them around and turned Alex's brains to mashed potato.

I sat in my cell having a smoke. Sometimes generals don't have to fire the bullets, and just move in the troops.

Slim was my friend. We both are still alive. Alex is dead. That's how it works. Churchill and Stalin. The Poms had no time for the Frogs, and vice versa, but they fought together in two world wars against the Hun. Enough lessons from the past.

If you don't get it by now, pay for cable TV and watch the history channel.

It is 7 July 2000, as I sit at the kitchen table. Before we moved the kitchen table to where it is now, we hung Victor, our canary, in his cage from the ceiling. Now I get canary seed, water and feathers fluttering down on me as I write.

The *Chopper* movie is about to launch next month and the media frenzy is heating up. I received a nice letter from Eric Bana and some nice offers from all of those honest media people who don't pay criminals. Renee Brack has made an appearance in my movie. They rang and asked me if I'd mind if she put her head in on it.

I told them I've got no problem with her head. No pun intended. Renee was a good scout and she always came prepared. But there were many other media types who dangled their careers off the end of my criminal record. Let me put it another way. The amount of non-event, all dreams, no-talent media bums that have latched on to me to get themselves started is astonishing.

They forget and so do the public, but the bloke with no ears has done more for more people than a lot of people realise or would like to confess to. Good luck to Renee Brack. I hope her bit part in my movie kicks her on.

The media ring me with 'Chopper this' and 'Chopper that'. They come down to see me. They want photographs and autographs. The girls of the media strut in to see poor old Mark as if they are on the catwalk. All legs and push-up bras.

Then the cameras go on. Gone are the winks and the throaty laughs. Now it's hair in a bun, judgemental comments about money from crime and the poor victims. Blah blah blah.

It's all a show and I'm the dancing bear. I don't mind because every time they slag me my book sales go up. The more they pretend to hate me the more the public want to know what's going on.

I suspect the movie will enter the Kubrick world of *A Clockwork Orange* and be remembered by people who have never even seen it.

Billy the Texan once said to me that I was without a shadow of a doubt the greatest psychological manipulator of the media in Australian criminal history, but the same people dismiss me as not much of a crook compared to their great selves, of course. My idea of a successful criminal isn't much different from a successful anything else: someone who ends up with wealth, power, fame and long life.

Few crooks gain power, very few gain fame and even fewer gain long life. So a crook who has gained wealth, power, fame and long life is the winner – no contest.

Good crooks are never known. They have power and money without the fame. Serial killers get the fame with no power and no money and, usually, a lifetime behind bars. Violent criminals have a certain power, but only until they lose their strength, then they either reform or die. Some just get out of jail and become hairdressers like William John O'Meally.

I had fame, power and not much money. I can tell you that writing about crime is a hell of a lot better than committing it. That's why crime reporters tend to live longer than the criminals they write about. Except if they die of mixed grill and beer poisoning.

I'm a forward thinker. I'm not so worried about today's opinion but of tomorrow's and I suspect new generations will view this no-eared freak with a kinder heart than the mice who roar at me today. History has shown us that.

Speaking of mice, one of Beethoven's critics from the media, a name I forget, contacted a former Victoria Police detective inspector who, in turn, rang me. As a favour to the former inspector, I rang the mouse, or mousette. She was doing an article on me, the movie and so on.

I tried to explain that all the money that was due to me from the movie had already been signed over to a children's hospital cancer foundation, but she didn't want to know this, as the fact that I'd already given the movie money away to charity flew in the face of her 'how criminals make money from crime' articles. Again, it's an example of how the truth is never believed. People would rather believe the lie.

All she wanted was a black story, so she didn't want a white answer. She only wanted the legend, the myth and the lie – and anything that wavered from what she had already planned on writing was, to her, a lie. She intended to turn her version into reality by printing it, then it would become the 'truth'. That is, the truth to a vast number of her unsuspecting readers.

I was too polite to mention that the only person making any money at the time was her. I wasn't being paid for the interview and she was getting plenty. I've seen a lot of hypocrisy and dishonesty and a lot of rackets in my time, but I've never seen more hypocrisy and dishonesty than there is in the media racket. They're geniuses at it.

I once said to my publisher many years ago that when you jump on the horse you flog her till she drops. It is now July 2000 and, as I write this, the media storm over the *Chopper* movie is already beginning to break.

I said to my publisher over the phone, 'Get off the piss and edit this book.' Then I said, 'Remember that horse I first mentioned to you – well, we are standing in the barn and the horse has bolted and no bastard is riding it.'

It's too late, Frankenstein's monster has left the castle and we are all hiding under the table. The myth that we created has escaped into the world of reality and nothing and no one can bloody well put the genie back in the bottle. Have I mixed enough metaphors for you? I don't even know what a metaphor is but it sounds good, doesn't it?

It was then that the psychology that I've often tried to explain truly hit home. It was like when I was in the Pink Palace, Risdon Prison in Tasmania. Inmates all around me are cutting off their ears, and there are riots, sit-ins and stop-works, suicides and unexplained insanity and the only quiet, polite prisoner in the jail was the only one they never blamed for any of it.

But I was the only one who could control it. That was mass psychology and you had to be in a prison for many years to understand the thinking and to be able to use the psychology to your own gain. To control any situation, even a mass situation like a prison population, you must use psychology, not violence or force of arms. Yes, indeed, violence and force of arms is a vital tool, but that's all it is. Psychology is the guiding force.

Violence, or the threat of it, is the bullet. But the gun that directs the force is the psychology of fear.

No one ever believed that the mass hysteria of a whole prison population could be caused by one man.

They were frightened of me, yet, at the same time, not frightened. That is one of the greatest tricks. They know you are dangerous, but they don't feel any personal danger, as I've always allowed the other fellow to have his ego and to feel superior to me physically, yet inferior to me mentally. As long as I allowed the other fellow his feeling of physical superiority, while maintaining his subconscious sense of mental and emotional inferiority, he would do what I wanted. He would use his physical strength to get the approval of the man he believed was his mental superior.

It is not a perfect science and some of those I tried to control could turn on me. I've been attacked countless times but it was always my reaction afterwards that enabled me to turn an attacker into a friend. I stabbed Alex and later we became allies. He turned on me and he became dead.

I don't know what Freud would think about it but his ink blots

43

wouldn't have mattered much inside H Division, although I must admit there was a touch of what Sigmund called penis envy when I dropped my strides. The quickest way to analyse an inmate in there was to hit him in the head with a spade, an experiment allegedly performed by a large, no-eared man on one Richard Mladenich. But I digress.

It's all very Dr B F Skinner, the Black Prince of the 20th century on the dark side of behavioural psychology. He carried out behavioural-science tests on his own daughter, what we call mind games. She later took her own life, casting Skinner into the sin bin. However, his evil genius in relation to the study of mass psychology and behavioural science has been used by various governments during warfare. The CIA used Skinner's thinking during the middle and later stages of the Cold War. Make the other fellow doubt himself is the first rule and, since everyone is riddled with self-doubt, Skinner's psychological method for breaking down the emotional strength of the enemy was popular with the Cold War warriors. It's like all great science, simple to put into practice – if you have the weapons.

Enough said, however, on B F Skinner. I spent 17 years reading his work. Do you think I am about to toss that sort of in-depth study into a paperback? A teacher asks the question, the student provides the answer. The fact that I have provided some answers for you doesn't mean that I intend to provide them all. If I were to tell you all the secrets, it would be like giving a loaded gun to a child. The consequences could be bloody.

I was big and tough, with a taste for violence and a capacity to take pain. But what made me different was that I was prepared to learn from history. While the others were watching the races, I was reading about the great generals and their battles. I was able to use their lessons in the Australian underworld. I would smile and behave the fool but I would always remember what I had learned and use it against my enemies and, sometimes, my friends. You must remember that my enemies were often not that smart. Many of them thought the Battle of the Bulge was a fight in a strip club.

But I was just one of the biggest fish in a small septic pond. We were all dying by degrees. Many of my type were murdered, others died from their wounds, while others just rotted to become shadows of their former selves while in prison.

I retired, not to the front bar of some pub, but to the library where I began to write. It was not part of a master plan. We thought we might get one book out. It became a bestseller. Now this is the tenth, and I suspect the last, book I will write. My life has been made into a movie. It is all unbelievable.

The truth is, I got away with murder in the underworld and I got away with murder in the literary world.

I look into the fire and wonder why. Then I remember I will have to clean up all the ash in the morning.

CHAPTER 4

MIND GAMES

people fear what they
don't understand.

THERE are basically three sorts of crime: Unorganised Crime – lawless activity by individuals; Disorganised Crime – lawless activity by gangs; and Organised Crime – lawless activity by gangs, crews, teams, cartels, syndicates, call them what you will.

The Mafia is a continuing, never-ending tree of criminal conspiracy to gain economic power via physical force and private corruption. It is kept alive with the falling-leaf attitude. Each member is only a leaf, the roots of the tree are in place and so is the trunk. The leaves that do or don't blow off (or get blown away) won't affect the health of the tree itself. I've chainsawed big trees down and watched new suckers spring from the old tree's original root system. Any organised criminal group that has not been cut down within its first generation of life will never be cut down, as the root system after the first generation has taken hold. Any group who can trace its roots back 300 years or even 30 years is cemented in place.

Leaves may fall but the tree will remain. Any police or media remark to the contrary is rubbish, pure and simple. We should also remember that some police and the (very) odd journalist have been members of a crime family or two.

I'm not saying that criminal activity is a myth or nonsense; it is all very real, dangerous and deadly serious, be it unorganised, disorganised or highly organised or spur-of-the-moment thoughtless madness. You are just as dead if you're shot by some idiot with a crime fantasy and a stolen .22 pea rifle as you are if blown away by a marksman hired by a crime cartel using a state-of-the-art, high-powered sniper rifle that can take out a buffalo at two miles. What I'm saying is that this psychology of fear is an important tool used at all levels of criminal activity and, one day, the crime fighters and people who report on crime will come to understand this tactic.

I feel at times the police and the various news media to a certain degree do understand the fear myth I've outlined and they themselves use this very tactic to frighten governments via the general public. Budget funding relies heavily on public demand for more police to fight serious crime. The news media is not a public charity – the more the media can frighten the public the more newspapers they can sell and viewers they can attract. TV news and current affairs and crime documentaries rely heavily on this same psychology. The old Chinese proverb of killing one to scare ten thousand is very true and much used by all parties involved: cops, robbers, reporters and the humble spectator. They shiver in fright and vote with their minds, hearts and wallets to protect themselves from a monster that is largely a phantom of disinformation.

People fear what they don't understand and keeping the general public in a state of semi-ignorance is an important tool in the battle plans of both the good guys and the bad guys.

We work together to keep the square-heads in the dark. Politicians win, because they get votes from being tough on crime; coppers win, because they get more money and influence; and the media win because they have more stories to tell and sell. The crooks also win, in a way, because they become more feared.

Know this and believe it because the bloke writing this has mastered and used this very tool for well over 20 years. For once, the humble reader is being invited to look behind a closely guarded and secret door only to find the monster is mostly imagination. It is all a Hollywood production.

There is no one in the audience ... we are all up on the stage.

As always, my writing gets sidetracked. Because the *Chopper* film is out, all I seem to be doing is giving radio, TV, newspaper and magazine interviews. The movie has already been sold to the Russians, Japanese and Poms, and the rest of the English-speaking world are raving about it.

Andrew Dominik, the director, has turned out to be a cross between Stanley Kubrick and Doctor Strangelove. Eric Bana is on his way up. The fact that he is so great in this movie is further proof that I am a genius. I must modestly confirm the story others have told that I was the one who originally picked him for the role. They were talking about Russell Crowe at the time, but I couldn't understand why. He may have been a good Fitzroy ruckman, but as an actor I think he is fairly average.

I always thought Eric had what it took to do the business. After all, he comes from the northern suburbs, too, and can talk the talk. And he's got a sense of humour, and can tell a yarn, which is more than of these other poofy actors can. Anybody who wants to argue with my theory should look at Billy Connolly's film roles.

Then there were the offers from the BBC to do a documentary and requests from artists to sit for them for the Archibald Prize art contest. I've knocked back a list of wombats, including one offer involving serious money, to star in an Australian-made porn movie. They always said I was a tosser, but I didn't want to prove it.

Marriage and a young son bring with it certain rules and moral regulations, but fame, if you can call it that, does bring with it an odd sort of power and influence.

I had written two film scripts in Risdon Prison, 'Sing a Song of Sixpence' and 'The Band Played On'. I sent them off to the usual suspects, movie and TV people in Australia. Tait Brady at Palace Films, Michele Bennett, Andrew Dominik and various TV people. I thought for fun that I'd send one of each to my friend Sam Risovich in Reno, Nevada. Within a week, Sam rang me and said, 'Hey, Chopper, where do I send the money?'

My books are popular on the black market in various parts of America and they had the video of the movie in Reno before it was released in Australia. It was only my intervention that prevented the whole movie being downloaded on to the internet, something to do with an m-peg file, whatever that is.

I would like to see my film scripts – or at least one of them – on the big screen in Australia.

Everything is done in a hurry in America. The cash is arranged within days and they want to know when you plan to start production. When I said to Sam that it would take at least two years and explained that the Australian movie took nearly eight years to get off the ground, he nearly dropped the phone. But, like my books, producing a movie using one of my own scripts *will* happen, in spite of my critics.

As they say in Sicily, 'The Devil has a bank book too.' I won't explain the meaning of that proverb to you. Figure it out for yourself.

Sometimes I am amazed at the name 'Chopper Read'. I can talk to people I don't know and say it's Mark Read, and it's all very ho hum, but when I say 'Chopper' it's a different matter. I went to the Men's Gallery nightclub to empty out my pool table on a Friday lunchtime and met a young blonde, all tits and legs, blow-up-doll dancer named Shelley Hamilton-Smith. Just a 19-year-old cute kid who mentioned that one day she'd like to be a photographic model.

I rang Dave Lornie, the editor of *100% Home Girls* magazine, and, bingo bango, Miss Hamilton-Smith is a photographic model. Sometimes it's nice to be nice and being Chopper Read doesn't mean that you have to hurt everyone you come into contact with. These days I find myself doing more good turns for people than bad turns. It's a nice feeling to help someone out.

Maybe being a dad has mellowed me, I don't know. I guess I'm trying to be a better person. That doesn't mean I'm no longer the man I was. I will always remain that man. The leopard doesn't change his spots, but he does get older and he does grow tired and slower. Kindness is still treated as a weakness, human nature hasn't changed that much, but I've dropped my guard a hell of a lot. I guess Mary Ann and little Charlie have done that for me. I don't want to go all mushy but it's true.

Renee Brack from Showboat Productions wants to do another interview with me. The one she did for *Hard Copy* in 1991 and the stories and rumours surrounding that weekend nearly destroyed her TV career. She made an appearance in the movie – Renee Brack as herself – only after Michele Bennett rang and asked me if I didn't mind. People get me all wrong. They sting me, I sting them back, but I don't take it personally.

Business is business, sometimes it's in people's business or career interest to dump on me. I will survive, I will come back, and I always do so. Name three of Beethoven's critics – it's a very true saying. I'm expecting Elle McFeast to ring next. I'm not expecting a call from Alan Jones – not unless he wants to spend a penny. Life is funny, I'm writing a tenth book and trying to work out how I can make a movie as well while doing a third CD with Colin Dix, in between changing nappies and helping with Charlie.

At times it can be quite surreal. Thank God that I've been living on a farm, although nobody can be sure how long that will last for me. I have found that the farm injects normality into an otherwise insane world.

I've now got quite a list of bimbo TV reporters who have lost their jobs with this or that network contacting me regarding doing a TV documentary. Of course, I'm a retard and I swallow it hook, line and sinker. The trick is to get me to say yes and then they run away screaming that they have me nailed down for an interview. They then try and squeeze 25 or 30 grand out of one of the networks for this so-called, in-depth documentary.

I had this one lady say to me that she was having dinner and drinks with some big-deal network yuppie. All she had to do was argue the price with him. Strangely enough, she said, 'He's the same arsehole who sacked me several years ago.'

I listened in silence then said, 'Do you reckon you can pull it off?'

She laughed and said, 'I think I'll have to do a fucking bit more than pull him off, Chopper.'

I wasn't making a sexual joke or pun but this chick is the sort that jumps on every turn of phrase and comes back with a sexual jest. It was like having a telephone conversation with a dial-a-dirty-phone-call sex number. She purrs over the phone.

How am I meant to take it with TV chicks who say it straight out to me, 'I know you're a married man now with a wife and baby boy, but Jesus, Chopper, if you could agree to this I'd promise you more than a few bob in a brown paper bag. I won't beg but I will get on my knees and while I'm down there I'll blow your ears off.'

They forget, of course, that my ears have already been blown off. So there is no way I can respond to their kind but misguided offers. I think there is a whole underclass TV world of former TV girls who got the sack because they got a year too old or wouldn't blow the boss and are now willing to do anything if it puts some wind back into their sails.

Frank Sinatra was right when he called some of the media people whores and thieves. I've met more foul-mouthed, cock-teasing whores, sluts and low-life molls in TV land than in any brothel. I used to be innocent in these matters, but I got a rude shock. It's not a case of will they suck, it's a case of have you got a driver's licence, Chopper?

'Yes,' I replied to one lady. 'Why?'

'Because I can't give you head if I'm driving,' she answered.

I must admit there was some logic in that and I had to do what I could to keep the road toll down. Of course, all their deals fall through and the sexy phone calls stop.

But if you told a donkey about some of these TV, pay-TV and cable-TV ladies he would kick you in the head for telling lies. The stories are true, but so hard to believe Linda Lovelace wouldn't swallow them. Ha ha.

Russell Crow ... they wanted him to play me
in the film. I could never work out why.

CHAPTER 5

SLAUGHTER IN THE PEN

I met a bloke who was
always paranoid that he was going
to be murdered, so I shot him.

I CAN'T sleep. I live on a diet of Melbourne Bitter beer, XNAX anti-panic tablets, Panadeine Forte, painkillers and sleeping pills, yet I can't get to sleep until three o'clock every morning. I'm up as early as 6.30 chopping wood, chainsawing, feeding the chickens, feeding my birds, my two cats and two dogs – Little Bill, my Jack Russell, and Patsy Cline, a.k.a. Patsy Crime, my Staffordshire bull terrier-heeler cross. Patsy has turned out to be a formidable guard dog and very protective of home and family.

We had to shoot more than 60 of the chickens and pen up the pure breeds. My brother-in-law, Jan Blyton (no relations to Enid) and Shane Farmer did the dirty deed with a .22 rifle and a .410 shotgun. Naturally, I didn't take part. Not only do I have a well-documented dislike of bloodshed, my application to have my firearm prohibition order lifted was still being considered by Police Commissioner Richard McCreadie and the firearm registry office. I will haunt them until it's lifted.

I got a phone call from New York from former Detective Inspector 'Rocket' Rod Porter over an upcoming story in *Ralph* magazine. He didn't wish to hurt my feelings and *Ralph* magazine was giving me the right of reply. I don't wish to hurt him. It is funny how throughout all our past history, not all of it good, we have remained friends. Former Detective Sergeant Steve 'Dirty Larry'

Curnow was with him. How they got visas to get into anywhere other than Sing Sing is beyond me.

They wouldn't tell me their business but, in jest, asked if I knew anyone in New York. I said only a guy named Tommy Caprice, but when I told him to go to an address in Little Italy, Mulberry Street, Rod said, it 'sounds like something out of a Mafia movie'. He wasn't far wrong but, as always, people generally think I'm pulling their leg.

I also know a guy in New Jersey and the Central Bronx district – old school friends from Thomastown state school. All Italian and all connected up to their back teeth. But what would I know, I'm just a chicken farmer with no firearm licence and international crime connections.

The underworld murder rate has dropped off in Melbourne. I rang a few people and complained that my tenth book depended on at least three to four more good hits.

'Oh, great, Chopper. I'll just run out the fucking door now and kill a few more just so you can write another book. And when they make a movie about it they can leave me out of that one too!' was the reaction of one old friend. He was quite offended that he was left out of the *Chopper* movie. In fact, he wanted to staple gun Michael Gudinski's top lip to his nose he was so pissed off. It's all a bit funny, two of the biggest professional hit men in Australia are now so offended that they got left out of the *Chopper* movie. So offended they are on strike – in protest, they aren't going to kill any more people. Now, there is a unique form of protest. The whole thing is quite insane. Hit men with hurt feelings who have agreed not to kill certain people because they know I'd only write about it, and they want to punish me. Well, it's working. I needed their hits to be a big hit. It's quite frustrating, as my books do depend on bullets and big tits, as I am sure any literary reviewer could tell you. The big tits I can get, but hit men going on strike for artistic reasons! If you made a movie about that or tried to tell that story and get anyone to believe it, you'd be out of luck. So I feel safe in repeating it because you're just not going to believe it anyway.

That's the magic of my writing. They say little or any of it is believed, yet it's read by many. You figure it out. I can't.

Saturday, 16 September 2000

An artist called Suzanne Soul came down with a lady photographer to draw me and take about a thousand photos to help her prepare to paint me for the Archibald Prize art competition. Suzanne is 4'10" tall in the old money and a cute little weapon when she isn't doing ladies hairdressing. It was all a bit surreal — if only I knew what that meant.

We met out on my farm, her and her photographer Jody Hutchinson. The wind was blowing and a sort of 'this isn't happening' madness set in. The wind has that effect on me. It's the same with horses — spooks them and makes them do wild things.

I'm weather-beaten and weary at the sight of little cuties but my brother-in-law Jan Blyton and my wife's cousin Warwick Golding couldn't help but notice that Suzanne was not totally ugly. I'm a bit jaded in this area and also realise that being a 46-year-old, out-of-shape middle-aged man with his lovely wife and baby son six metres away places me right out of the game.

It's a bloody pity other fellows my age don't wake up to reality. That's all I can say. No names mentioned, no pack drill, as my dear old dad would say. It wouldn't matter if Miss Head Job 1999 walked through the door. I've got this 'been there, done that a thousand times' attitude. All I want is to get with the programme. Do the business, whatever the business is, unless it is funny business, and piss off. No offence, but I don't attempt to relive some second sexual childhood, dancing about like a two-year-old with his dick in his hand and his foot in his mouth — or the other way around if you are double-jointed.

Nevertheless, embarrassments aside, Suzanne was ultra-professional and I suspect if she doesn't win the Archibald, she will one day be recognised as an artist of some note. But what would I know, I'm just an interesting model with no ears and a criminal record as long as your arm, not to mention something else as long as your arm.

Speaking of lovelies, Shelley Hamilton-Smith and her yummy little mate got photographed for that award-winning publication *100% Home Girls* men's magazine, as I had arranged. They were surprised when I told them I wanted no favour in return. They had been victims of this no one does anything for anyone without wanting something in return business. It left the two young ladies somewhat puzzled when they came across a true gentleman like my good self. A little like Professor Henry Higgins, not to be confused with that scallywag Buck Higgins.

I'm due to take part in a BBC documentary on gambling. They want to talk to me about the insane game of Russian Roulette, which I used to play with the Albanians and Vietnamese in Footscray in 1987. I have to go to Melbourne for the day and I'm not happy. I've become agoraphobic beyond the farm and Richmond, Tasmania. This means that I get concerned and uneasy when I leave my home patch.

It's a little like a lot of farmers who are down here. They suffer from their own form of agoraphobia. They are frightened of agriculture, so they don't do much of it. I don't even like going to Hobart once or twice a week and I dread leaving the state of Tasmania. No fear involved, but I keep thinking the plane will crash one day and with my luck I'll be in the fucking thing. That's not fear – that's mindless paranoia.

But planes never crash, do they? And a fear of flying is only mindless stupidity, isn't it? Totally baseless, mindless nonsense, stupid paranoia. Planes never fall out of the sky or run into mountains or tall buildings. It's all in the mind. Take another pill, you paranoid bastard. Hypochondriacs never get sick and paranoid people never die.

I met a bloke who was always paranoid that he was going to be murdered, so I shot him. I met another bloke who always thought someone would set him up. Now he's doing 20 years. I met a copper who was always worried he couldn't pay his mortgage, so he joined the drug squad, and that solved all his problems – for a while. I think he's got a few headaches just now.

The graveyards only take fit and healthy young people with not a care or fear in the world. Yeah, pig's arse.

The BBC doesn't pay for interviews. Oh dearie me, no. They said they would fly me to Melbourne and back again, plus buy me a lovely lunch. I wanted to tell them that they sell food in Tassie, too; I might get them to fly here. Buddy Holly, the Big Bopper and I can meet them at the airport. I've reached the stage where I don't need any extra publicity. There is no thrill in not being paid to do an interview and being asked to go out of my way to do it.

This is the song they all sing and I'm turning tone deaf. Has a ring to it these days that I can no longer hear. Let Mohammed come to the fucking mountain − with his chequebook. Or, better still, US dollars. Why should I be asked to go to the time and effort and my own personal expense, so that some team of pricks that I don't even know can make money? Oh, but it's good publicity.

Yeah, Chopper Read really needs to get his fucking photo taken yet again. I mean, I wake up in the morning and say to myself, 'Gee, I wish I could get my photo taken or someone to put a bit more shit on me in a newspaper or magazine article.' I need that. Or be asked to take part in another 'no money for me' film or documentary and then to be made to look like a raving mental case after the editing. People cut out all the nice bits and leave in all the bad bits. Come to think of it, that's what I did with a cutthroat razor and a tied-up drug dealer.

The media pussies always say, 'Don't worry, Chopper, we won't be doing a hatchet job on you.' No, of course not. Media people no longer use hatchets; they use large, sharp knives that they plunge deep into your back after they wave you goodbye.

So that's that, I've just talked myself out of going to Melbourne for the BBC documentary. Let the cheap bastards come here and pay me nothing. Travelling over to Melbourne for nothing except the promise of a free lunch is starting to make no sense whatsoever. The BBC comes all the way from London, then they want me to fly to Melbourne to meet them. Pig's arse.

Next topic.

Every writer reaches a point when there is nothing left to say. I reached this point after my first book and said only a little more in the next eight books following the first. I've had writer's block and tackle, especially tackle. (It's well known that women go for novelists because of their writer's tackle.) I thought I had something to say in this book, but I've realised yet again my mind has wandered away on its own and got totally lost.

It's hard to hold the memory cells together with Charlie running around the place with a pot trying to hit the cat on the head and the two dogs fighting outside which has forced one of the stray fowls to jump up through the open kitchen window. This has forced Charlie to chase the fowl and the cat to jump up on the kitchen table while I'm trying to write this.

Did Hemingway have to put up with this? Maybe he did and that's why he topped himself with his favourite shotgun. Personally, I would find that a little too messy for the next-of-kin.

Now I know why I could put a book together so quickly in prison. I had nothing else to do except write (and bash people). I rang my dad and he spent 20 minutes talking to me about bowel movements. I have learned that old people do that. This was an STD phone call and he didn't talk about anything else in a 20-minute conversation.

Life for me has taken some odd twists and turns. I'm publicly hated and privately loved. It is thought to be politically correct to publicly condemn me as a criminal who profits from crime yet privately say nothing when I donate large sums of money to a children's cancer charity.

I will try to give you one example of the many odd contributions that go to make up the fabric of my life today. A friend of mine, Shane Farmer, the Tasmanian nightclub king, is also an Australian Labor Party (ALP) backroom boy, as the expression goes. Another mate, Charles 'Charlie T' Touber, is a music and rock and roll major event concert promoter. They form probably the most powerful double act in the Tasmanian hotel and nightclub industry.

Charles Touber once ran for the Senate on the ALP ticket and is also a local Labor Party behind-the-scenes operator, which comes in useful. Shane Farmer is big, loud and brash with the personality of an out-of-control chainsaw. Charles Touber is a doctor of political science, a quietly spoken gentleman, a deep thinker, a serious sort of chap with a sense of comedy not unlike a Monty Python undertaker.

In business, Charlie T is the velvet glove that Shane Farmer fills with a concrete fist. Farmer has all the diplomatic skills of a Nazi soap salesman touting for business outside a Jewish bathhouse, but his big mouth is only beaten by his big heart, thus meaning his good points outweigh his bad points.

Charlie T, on the other hand, is as smooth as silk, a gentleman with a great deal of polish and personal charm. Meaning that if I were to suffer a flashback and do a toe-cut job on either man, I would have selected Charlie T first. Farmer is as smooth as a barbed-wire fence. He would rather die than part with a penny. Touber would tell you where the money is, then tell you that Farmer has the combination to the safe. All in all, they are two tough nuts I'd rather have on side, as trying to crack the bastards would be a fucking nightmare.

Well, they are my mates and each in their own way is as complex as the writer of this story. Although, thank goodness, they don't have the same criminal record.

I'm someone that people from normal society try to avoid. No one really wants to be publicly linked to me. I'm like a shadow no one really wants behind them, not publicly at any rate. But privately, I find myself courted by many and various people. Many people come to me and want to chat but they are not overjoyed when they see a camera pointing in our direction after dark at a private function.

Such was the case at the exclusive premiere, private invitation, no cameras allowed, opening of the Wild West Sports Saloon at 251 Liverpool Street, Hobart. I found myself, through no fault of my own, mixing with half the political and old-money business heavyweights in Hobart town.

My rumoured involvement with Shane Farmer in the Men's Gallery strip club in Hobart had reached the stage where the more I denied it the more people believed it. This rumour naturally followed on to the Wild West Sports Saloon, which also includes a second club upstairs – The Viper Room. I found myself in the company of the Hon. Paul Lennon MHA, the Deputy Premier of Tasmania. Richard McCreadie, the Tasmanian Commissioner of Police, was also meant to attend. His son Scott McCreadie works for Shane and Charles at the club, which is also a good thing, as it's sometimes hard for young people to gain useful employment in Tassie. But back to Scott's father, the police commissioner … I'm told that if he did attend it was only after my camera and myself went home.

The background to this is that I've been having a comic running battle with McCreadie to have the firearm prohibition order on myself lifted. I always remember when Bob Hawke got in as Prime

Minister, they sang a song in Labour Party hotels: 'The working class can kiss his arse, Bob's got the foreman's job at last.'

In talking to the Deputy Premier I thought to myself, So this is the new face of Labour. But both sides of the political fence were represented at the opening, which is the fair and balanced thing to do. There were the new true believers and also a large collection of young Liberals in attendance, led by a lawyer turned political whatever called Andrew Gregson.

Young Gregson was a worthy opponent of mine when the university visited Risdon Prison to debate with the prison's Spartan Debating Team. He represented the university, in case you wondered. I was with the Spartans.

I noticed not a great deal of difference between the Labour and Liberal gathering. Neither group wanted to talk politics. Politicians rarely do after hours, as they may be asked a question for which they can't find the right answer.

I have always wondered why, with the American ships visiting Hobart regularly and such a wild nightlife, the economy is going down the toilet. This is a great place and should be the biggest tourist spot in Australia. The average Tasmanian public servant or politician couldn't organise a piss-up in a Cascade brewery. (Please note product placement: that should be good for a few slabs of stubbies.) The whole state is bankrupt, which means that the only economy that works is the black economy. The whole state is a political cripple being carried along by a kind-hearted nation.

The population of the state shouldn't even warrant a state government or the title of state. As for the politicians already in office, if they all shot themselves in the head tomorrow, no one would even notice. The businessmen of this state run the state. The politicians should go interstate before we are all die intestate.

In Tasmania, the business community provide the organ grinders, and the politicians are the monkeys. That's why, whenever a politician is invited to any function in Tasmania, peanuts are always served with the drinks.

Personally, I reckon Charles Touber and Shane Farmer and my good self could run the whole state with a pocket calculator and a mobile phone. We would make it the vice capital of the world. We would get rid of booze and cigarette taxes. We would introduce strip joints on every street corner, then get rid of death taxes.

Then we would start a massive international ad campaign to lure tourists and rich old settlers. Something like ... 'Come and bury yourself in the map of Tassie.' Could just work.

CHAPTER 6

WAVE GOODBYE, SURFERS

The Beach Boys killed God-only-knows how many.

I PUT the phone down. As often happens, I'm left in total disbelief. I was talking to my friend, 'The Italian', asking about the welfare of the three young surfer boys. 'They went swimming and drowned, Chopper,' he said. 'Hey, did you hear that Reggie Kray died?'

The first part of news was stunning, to say the least. The three young hit men, who went to make up the wave that knocked roughly 15 Melbourne criminal identities off their feet, had just been 'vanished' in one short sentence.

Before I could ask for more detail, I was hit with a second bit of news, which for sentimental reasons vastly outweighed the first bit of gossip. Reggie Kray, the last remaining brother of the Kray family and the firm that ruled the London underworld, was dead. They were my boyhood heroes.

First went Ronnie, Reggie's twin brother, then Charlie, the eldest of the brothers, and then Reggie, just 35 days after getting out of prison. He was put away in 1969 for murder. Bladder cancer – they couldn't take the piss out of him, even at the end.

What a way to go. I rang another friend for any sort of news regarding the Beach Boys. The Jew answered the phone.

'Did ya hear the news?' I asked.

'Yeah,' he replied, 'Reggie Kray died.'

'No,' I answered, 'the Beach Boys.'

'Fuck those junkies, Chopper, who cares?' He was always a sympathetic type.

'I do,' I said, 'I'm writing a book.' I was also the sympathetic type, as it happens.

'Jesus, you and your fucking books,' said my Jewish mate.

'What happened?'

'Reggie Kray is dead and all you can talk about is three dead faggot surfer boys,' said the Jew.

'What happened?' I asked again.

'Do you remember that old World War II Jap auto handgun your old man gave me for my twenty-first birthday?' My dad was a sympathetic type, too, but something didn't add up.

I thought for a moment. I did recall an old Japanese handgun that went missing from under my dad's bed around the time of the Jew's twenty-first birthday. At the time, the Jew denied any knowledge of the theft and my dad blamed me for taking the old war relic.

After the flashback, I said to the Jew that I sort of remembered the 'gift'.

'Well,' said the Jew, 'I don't have it no more.' He didn't have to say any more. For the Jew to give up a gun could mean only one thing. A bullet in a body could link you to murder – if the gun could be found.

I told the Jew, 'I'm going to have a death notice put in the London *Times* newspaper for Reggie Kray.'

'Do they still have a London *Times*?' he asked.

'Why? What happened to it?' I asked

'I don't know,' said the Jew. 'I think Rupert Murdoch bought it.'

'My dad's old gun?' I said.

'No, the London *Times* newspaper,' replied the Jew. 'What the fuck are you on about, Chop?'

'The Beach Boys,' I answered.

'Reggie Kray just died and all you want to talk about is them wombats. Fuck you.'

With that, he hung up. Just my luck, I thought to myself. Just when the biggest bit of criminal news hits, and me in the middle of my tenth book fucking desperate for details, Reggie Kray up and dies on me.

Bloody lovely. So what do I do now? Write a post mortem on

Reggie Kray? Meanwhile, three young hit men who would have killed more people in a month than the Kray brothers killed in a lifetime have gone on the missing list. And yet their death rated little more than a throwaway sentence in the face of the news of the great Reggie Kray's death.

This goes to show that it's not how many you've killed that counts, it's how famous you are for doing it that matters. Ronnie and Reggie killed one man each. The Kray brothers firm killed three men, four at the most, and wrote themselves into international criminal history.

The Beach Boys killed God-only-knows how many and died nameless, totally unknown outside of a small crew of men who not only created them but also destroyed them.

Generals have statues made after them. When soldiers die, they go into a lime-filled pit and are lucky if they get a white cross on the bare dirt.

I wondered why things had been a bit quiet in Melbourne of late. Oh well, anyway. Rest in Peace, Reggie.

Very often in the criminal world, news that should be of importance and the main topic of conversation is cast aside and a murder that happened half an hour before is forgotten because Collingwood have just been beaten by the Bulldogs by seven goals.

Such a loss is, of course, a totally shattering blow for all concerned — and, on this occasion, resulted in the dear departed, who had just been placed in the boot of the car along with a pick and a garden spade, being driven to a hotel and remaining in the boot in the car park while all concerned drank in the pub and talked about the football game.

At the end of the night, with all parties pissed, a taxi was called to avoid driving over the limit, because that would be illegal, then homeward for a good night's sleep and, upon waking, all parties were very much hungover and didn't remember where they have been drinking in the several pubs in Collingwood, Carlton, Fitzroy or St Kilda.

They had to cruise around the inner suburbs until the car was found. Well, you wouldn't want to leave it there too long before it would get a bit gamey.

Now get this, upon finding the car, they discovered it was parked in a private parking area near the pub and had been wheel-clamped, so the body had to be transferred from one car boot to another. Then, travelling across the Westgate Bridge, they got a flat tyre. Imagine getting the spare out of the boot, then the jack and various tools, while not allowing blocked traffic and passers-by to notice a body, plus a pick and a garden spade in the boot.

Luckily, it was the driver's front-side wheel, so the two police who pulled up to find out what was going on stood up front while the car was lowered and flat tyre, jack and tools were replaced in the boot.

That evening in the hotel, after the body had been burned in an industrial furnace, meaning the pick and spade were not needed, the topic of conversation was still on Collingwood's disgraceful defeat at the hands of Footscray. Believe it or not, it is a true story. I'm sure that if Mad Charlie was alive today he would be able to confirm the details.

When writing stories one must include the odd photo. From time to time I've been asked to submit a short story for various magazines and I've done so and included photos. The stories never saw the light of day and the photos were lost forever until recently, when a letter arrived from Miss Libby Noble, editor of Australian *Penthouse* magazine.

She had been going through old files belonging to the previous editor and come across a story and an old photo I thought had been lost forever, and she was kind enough to return the photo. I had planned way back to dedicate a book to my three late uncles Ronnie, Ray and Roy Read, but without the old family photo it wasn't a lot of use.

They were Collingwood boys from the old Collingwood push, and the photo, believe it or not, was taken at the bar at Luna Park, St Kilda, before World War II.

Ray is the bloke in the middle, Ronnie to his right, Roy to the left. The Japs cut off Ray's head at a place called Toll Plantation. The details are sketchy and my dad's memory isn't what it once was. He told me it was called the Toll Plantation massacre. The Japs murdered 11 men, mostly Dutch plantation owners and some AIF men. The Aussies then massacred 300 Japanese prisoners of war in retaliation, a secret not mentioned in dispatches. Funny, that. The Japs tied Ray's hands with string and fishhooks, a few loops around the wrists and a fishhook at each end. If the prisoner tried to break free, he would rip his own flesh. A neat little trick and a much-used one, a cheap and easy way to restrain a prisoner.

Evidently, it was an honour to be beheaded. Lesser men were simply shot, but my uncle had strangled several Japanese officers to death while trying to escape. The Japanese were most angry about this, yet very impressed at the damage one man could cause. He had buried the body of a Japanese major in the sand and would not tell the Japs where it was. He couldn't, as he had killed the major at night and buried him at low tide on the beach. During the day, it was high tide and Ray couldn't tell them where the body was even if he had wanted to.

They mistook his dumb silence for sheer bravery and, according to the Samurai code of Bushido, they gave Uncle Ray a fitting send-off. Apart from the way he ended it, Uncle Ray had led a pretty uneventful life.

Ronnie returned from the war with his right leg missing and would win foot races at the Collingwood Christmas sports events by running flat out then taking his false leg off and tossing it over the finishing line. It was his party trick. According to the rules, it was the first foot across the line that won. The RSL and the Collingwood Football Club sponsored most of these running events and were reluctant not to award Ronnie the trophy and ten-bob prize money, given the way he had lost his leg. In the end, they had to change the rules to include the word 'man' across the finish line and remove the word 'foot'. So much for Uncle Ronnie.

However, it was shy old Uncle Roy who was my favourite. He was the youngest of the three brothers, and he survived the Japanese prison camps by telling them he was a dentist. The Japs all had bad teeth and no dentist and Roy had a pair of stainless steel pliers he had pinched from somewhere. He was sent from prison camp to prison camp pulling out the teeth of Japanese.

In the end, he became quite good at it and returned to Collingwood and set himself up as a backyard dentist. Ah yeah, he'd say, it's no use drilling that tooth, it will just have to come out, and that would be that. Please pay at the door. You see, all Roy could do was pull teeth. He thought plaque was something you stuck on the wall. Eventually, he had to shut up shop after an accident with a bottle of chloroform that dropped off the mantelpiece in the kitchen and burned the house down when it hit the wood stove. At sixpence a tooth and between 10 and 20 a day – it was a nice little earner while it lasted.

He had a running battle with the Commonwealth Police and the army because he was listed as a deserter until his dying day. He never marched in an ANZAC parade. To be taken prisoner, then listed as a deserter, in spite of the fact that he was finally found in a prison camp on the infamous Burma railway, never sat well with Uncle Roy. Although he never pulled the teeth of any Aussie soldier, he would pull out teeth for any British officer. He was quite feared among the Japanese, who never showed their fear. The Japs could take pain and would say no to any form of painkiller – not that there was much to hand. In spite of blinding pain, they would not utter a cry, mutter or murmur.

Uncle Roy learned that a dentist was a much-feared fellow. He quite enjoyed pretending to be a dentist and would always state his occupation as 'dentist' to the end. The funny thing was that he died of blood poisoning from a mouth full of rotten teeth that went septic.

Having seen the pain he inflicted on others, he never went near a dentist himself. Not much of a story but they are almost forgotten uncles and there is only one photo to remember them by. So thanks, Libby Noble, for returning it.

Every book I write is my last. As I have mentioned before, my publishers and I share a comic remark that when you jump on the horse you flog her till she drops. The old horse has stumbled a good many times and tossed us off many times more. But we can get back on and keep on going. Now we jest that the poor old girl only has three legs and no rider but she is still charging up the hill. But soon she will be out of sight, and so this really will be my last. I think.

Anyway, because of this I am digging up old family history to get it down on paper. My son, Charlie Vincent, may read this one day and so I feel I must tell you of my great-uncle Eammon Euon Read whose claim to fame was shooting his CO during the famous 1916 Easter uprising in Dublin, Ireland. Rubin Read, Eammon's elder brother, was a hero who fought with the great Michael Collins and

Eamon De Valera, but Eammon, whose name was spelled incorrectly by the drunken doctor who delivered him, was one of the greatest cowards the IRA ever had. He was famous for shooting both British troops and his own men while escaping any tight situation. When Great-Uncle Eammon finally left the IRA, Michael Collins put a price on his head. However, it was believed that cunning old Eammon got in first and outlived Collins.

Sounds like me and poor fat Alphonse.

You see, the Reads belonged to a small group of Protestants who fought along with the Catholics against the British for a free Ireland before it turned into a religious issue.

Great-Uncle Eammon went on to become an informer for the hated black and tans who fought against the IRA, and then De Valera put a price on Great-Uncle Eammon's head himself. After three failed attempts to shoot De Valera, Uncle Eammon shot four black and tan soldiers in an attempt to frame his nemesis for murder. He went on to become a communist and, according to the family legend, along with Rial Regan and Tommy Taylor, he is believed to be one of the original founders of the Irish National Liberation Army, the feared and shadowy INLA. After acting as a hired gun for the INLA and renegade breakaway units of the IRA, he was still informing for the British, the Ulstermen and the armed unit of the Orange Lodge.

Mind you, Great-Uncle Eammon changed his name and joined the British Army only to desert them in the face of African enemies. He changed his name again and fled to America and was shot dead when he was caught cheating in a poker game.

During his 44 years, legend has it, he married nine women, divorced none of them, escaped 18 times from three different prisons and assorted police and military lock-ups. You could say that Eammon was a VD-ridden alcoholic, lying, cheating, thieving, murdering coward and ladies' man, as well as a woman basher. And those were his good points.

As family history has it, he was the man who shot and nearly killed his elder brother Rubin after the British Army put a one-hundred-pound reward out on Rubin. After all, business is business. No wonder I didn't have a brother. Can you imagine two Reads trying to shoot each other?

Altogether, Great-Uncle Eammon was possibly the greatest arsehole the Read clan has, or will ever produce, which is no mean feat. Instead of hiding him away in the family skeleton cupboard, I'd like to bring him out, dust him off and say with pride, 'Great-Uncle Eammon, I salute you.' My dad always told me that the Read clan boasted worse arseholes than his boy Chopper.

What sort of dad would I be if I didn't include a photo of my son Charles Vincent, little Chop Chop? My old mate Doug Young gave Charlie a toy wooden hammer, which was a nice thought. However, with child safety in mind, I had bought a second-hand 240GL Volvo, and Charlie would sit in the back in his booster safety seat and proceed to bang the hammer against the window. The oven door had already been given a damn good seeing-to along with the two cats, Poop Foot and Ernie, and our two dogs, Little Bill and Patsy Cline.

The hammer caper was getting quite out of hand for a while there. Charlie is a strong kid for a mere 13 months of age. As I write this, he is quite a size and weight. He can pick up a solid-iron fire poker that weighs about 2.5 kilos with one hand and swing it about the kitchen, laughing his head off. The dogs run for cover and I have to disarm Charlie and say, 'No Charlie, no poker.' Charlie looks at me, laughs and runs for his little wooden hammer and, while Daddy isn't looking, WHACK, he lets me have a rather hefty blow to the kneecap. Don't tell me kneecapping runs in the family.

So into the fire the hammer went. He looks up towards his official Tee Ball baseball bat that hangs from the kitchen ceiling, laughs, then runs off. All Charlie seems to do is eat and laugh, when he's not bashing me up. He likes to begin breakfast with a bloody great bowl of custard and Weetabix all mashed up with toast and vegemite. He has six teeth (which is two more than me) and munches away on the toast until his whole face is covered in vegemite.

The dogs look on, waiting for Charlie to drop his toast, but at 13 months he can read their minds. It's Charlie's toast and no one else's, except, of course, if Charlie's attention is drawn to Mary Ann opening up his tin of custard and pulling out the Weetabix, then Charlie stands transfixed, watching the main event being prepared.

While this is going on, Little Bill comes out of hiding and creeps over and gently snatches the toast from Charlie's hand, and then the fun begins. We had to hang Charlie's plastic baseball bat up as well.

I won't continue, as I will start to sound like one of those proud dads who think every move his son makes is brilliant. Plus, the RSPCA may not be happy to know what a little Read can do to a dog he suspects of illegal use of his vegemite toast.

It's good being a dad and I must say that when Charlie was born it changed my whole life. Strange words coming from a man with my reputation. Hard to believe, I know. I just hope we can make it last.

I hope that, because I have come to this so late in life, I am able to understand it more. I have seen more violence than most men who have not been to war. I have planned the death and destruction of my enemies. I have inflicted great pain on people and then gone off for eight hours' sleep. I have cut off people's toes and then had a feed of fish fingers. Yummy. I have had people cry and beg for help. And that is only my book editors, who have been reduced to gibbering wrecks. The reason I was feared in the underworld was that I had no fear. There were men who were stronger than me, but none was as dangerous. I was not frightened to die and my enemies knew that.

They had more troops, more guns and more money, but they were frightened to fight because they couldn't afford to lose. I didn't care if I lived or died, so I was the most dangerous of all. Like a wolverine, which is a small animal, but nothing in nature will mess with it because it has no fear. Polar bears won't take it on.

I made a decision never to marry or have children while I was at war. I would not have a weak spot that my enemies could exploit. A family man was a dead man in the crime world. You could always get at him through his family.

When I met Mary Ann, I had already retired from crime. To go from the fog of my former life to a new start was something I didn't believe could ever happen.

The only sad thing for my son is that his dad will always be remembered for the things he once did and the man he once was. Forgetting that all of us used to be someone else who did other things than they do today, once upon a time. The cross that I carry is that, until my dying day and beyond, I will always be seen as the man I once was and what came later will mean nothing compared to that. We all have a cross to carry – mine is that I used to be Chopper Read.

I can put the Chopper Read mask on when I need to. It entertains some and shocks others. But it is like putting on a uniform to go to work. I take it off when I get home to my family.

To the world I am a mad killer. To Charlie, I am just Daddy.

It is a burden he will also have to carry one day. When I go to parent–teacher nights, will the others see me as a dad or as a monster? Will parents let their kids come and play here, knowing I am the responsible adult looking after them? The truth is, I can look after kids because I know all the dangers in the world and then some.

I worry for Charlie. Everywhere he goes, he will be Chopper's son and will not be able to hide. I am covered with tattoos, have no ears and am now known around the world. Don't get me wrong. I don't mind the infamy but I worry that my son will have to live with the costs.

In the underworld, I lived through the wars, got my scars and lived. My enemies are dead or hiding. They are in jail or have become pathetic junkies. They hate the fact that many of them are unknown by the world while Chopper Read is famous. But will Charlie learn to hate the name the way so many others have over the years?

Friends of mine from Melbourne have told me to expect a new wave of murders. At least three, including at least one with a Moran influence to it. However, my continued book writing conflicts with the inside info I now receive. For example, I know that a few jockeys may have put the 'mocker' on themselves by being too close to a few crooks. Loose lips sink ships and favourites. See if I'm right.

As all concerned know that whatever I'm told is written down, they know I won't betray their trust, but a certain resentment has built up. I won't visit Melbourne when invited to birthday parties, weddings, funerals and general get-togethers. Too public.

My own death would be a major score. I know that if I was shot dead book sales would go thought the roof, so if I am gunned down in a hail of bullets I would like to announce that my publishers should be put on the top of any suspect list.

I'm sad to say that the only people with any real chance of killing me are, in fact, my own friends. They are also the only people with anything to gain. A former criminal turned author with inside knowledge on certain people dating back 30 years is, to put it ever so politely, a major security risk.

The irony is that I am far more dangerous with a pen than a gun. As an author, I have always walked a fine line. I have told enough to let the world know what the crime world is really like. But no one has done any jail time from my nine books. Luckily, it is not a criminal offence to mix metaphors, strangle grammar and butcher punctuation, or I'd be back inside.

Because this could and probably will be my last book, I know that some crims, particularly friends, will be worried that I will make it a tell-all. I know where the bodies are buried – literally. I could drop bombshell after bombshell. I could have the homicide squad out with sniffer dogs and shovels. They would dig up everyone short of Elvis. Many would like to spill my guts before I spilled them myself.

Some insiders see me as a criminal historian and they ring me with information. They want to know that, if they die, someone will be able to record what really happened. They tell me what has happened and what will happen. Some of it is just rumour and theory. But it is amazing how much of it turns out to be true. I must also consider that I am being fed disinformation, although I do check and counter-check any and all inside information.

I don't need the CIA computer to analyse what is going on. I can smell death and the pong is coming over Bass Strait right now.

I will sit here and play with my son. Sooner or later, the phone will ring and it will be a friend or a reporter to tell me of the latest murder. Before he gives me the name, I will write down on a pad the name of the dearly departed. I will know who it is before his name has been officially released. I could ring people now and tell them they will be dead within months. They would see it as a threat. If the police were to find out, then I would end up on the suspect list. No, better not to interfere.

I will watch and wait. I see the names of some crooks in the papers. I wonder if they know they are dead men walking. Some of them don't know that their best friends are plotting their deaths. Have another short black, fellas. It is much later than you think.

I am now, however, no longer an active part of the life and the world that my old friends come from and still inhabit. Sentimental for old time's sake, friendships can only go so far and I now must face the fact that these friends now view me as an outsider, even though I helped to create some of the main players still involved.

Why should I continue to be given the before-it-happens information simply to help me write a book?

I haven't lost the ability to see into the minds and hearts of old friends. I can read the play too well and now I know that my once-upon-a-time best friend would, if I placed myself into his hands, kill me. He won't visit Tasmania because he rightly suspects that I've seen behind the smiling face and, if he visited Tasmania, I'd have to do him in. It would give me no pleasure. It would be self-defence. Yet, in the face of this discomfort, he still tells me things. I've sworn that if he dies before me I will write his true life story. His ego is so great that he must keep me informed, to a certain degree, so that if he gets either arrested or shot dead I will be the one to write his story.

That is the example of the sheer insanity of the world I write about. I write about it and the world that I once came from. It is also a situation so impossible to believe that, as the CIA used to say, 'We have believable denial on our side.'

Deniability – I can tell a true story so crazy that the reader simply will not believe it to be true. If you enter into a truth that no one will ever believe, you are protected by logic, as logic tells whoever reads or hears the story that it simply isn't true.

Don't believe it? Then think about this. After all I have done, I have never been convicted of murder. If you can use logic as a weapon to protect yourself, it is the best alibi you can have.

Believable deniability – that means, naturally, that the CIA had nothing to do with the Kennedy shooting. We all suspect they might have known a little more than the history books tell us, but we all deny they did it. This is what I write about – a truth so fantastic that it simply is not believed. I'm protected by the sheer insanity of a totally unbelievable truth. My friends are the people who really want to kill me and the truth they tell me is protected by the fact that no one believes it until after it happens and even then they still can't bear to face reality.

You're reading this and probably don't fully understand what I'm telling you. You sort of do but logic tells you it's all a lie, but you are sort of wondering if it could all be true. Magic, isn't it? Pure insane magic. When the truth shrouds itself in a cloak of lies it can walk among us totally unseen. Protected by the logic of believable deniability.

As my pen travels across the pages, I find myself moving further and further away from my original topic. The BBC interviewed me today. Newspapers and magazines in England have interviewed me. Miss Suzanne Soul, the cute little artist, has contacted newspapers about entering my portrait in the Archibald Prize art competition.

Miss Shelley Hamilton-Smith, the all-tits-and-legs young blonde dancer, grateful that I talked Dave Lornie, the editor of *100% Home Girls* magazine, into using her as a centrefold, has invited me to her engagement party. A strange way to say thanks, mate, I must say.

I'm being heavily pressured to actually make a movie based on one of the two film scripts I wrote. For Christ's sake, people in Reno, Nevada, are buying shares in the film script.

I don't have the faintest idea how to make a movie but it looks like I'm going to have to give it a try. I might start with a small documentary first. You don't need a lot of brains to make a documentary, all you have to do is interview a good handful of mental cases and Bob's your uncle. Considering that I'd interview active and retired hit men, I could call the documentary 'Bob's Your Dead Uncle'.

I used to collect the money out of the pool table in the Crown Bar at Shane Farmer's Men's Gallery nightclub but I got sick of signing autographs for drunks whenever I went in. The real reason I gave it away was that I don't like people knowing my movements, and arriving every Friday about midday to collect the money was an obvious risk. As a man who spent half a lifetime working out the movements of my enemies, I was not going to give them the same chance.

I was only making $100 a week and it wasn't worth the headache. The arrangement was that I'd handle public relations for his various business interests, nightclubs and so on for a regular sling. Public relations at times also included security. The truth is, I would rather shoot a loud-mouthed drunk than jolly him out of the building. In the end, none of it was worth the sheer pest value of the whole comedy of errors.

Friendship should never be mixed with money or business, not with me. I take people at their word and, if I feel I'm being short-changed, I have an overwhelming urge to shoot whoever I feel is short-changing me, and as a dad I can no longer do that sort of shit. Left to myself, I would rather deal with these matters at the Coroner's Court than the Bankruptcy Court. But I'm not by myself, so it's best to be friends and not worry about involving myself in other people's business affairs. The fact that everyone I know seems to drop my name with every second sentence they utter is just part of the cross I carry. I just have to live with it. That's life. Sure beats the alternative. I must say, as was pointed out to me by my wife, I wouldn't be mixing with the people I mix with today if Mad Charlie was still with me or any of my old crew. But I still get lonely.

I've got to have some form of social outlet, even if the people I talk to today wouldn't have got within 300 yards of me 15 or 20 years ago. The day of the hard man is over. Now we live in a world of limp-wristed, false pretending bullshitters and general flash Harry arsewipes.

As my dad still says, 'Too many dickheads, son, and not enough ammo.' How true. As Andrew Dominik, the now world-acclaimed director of the *Chopper* movie, pointed out, I am a contradiction, full of contradiction.

I'm quite enjoying the pleasures of Swedish motoring in my Volvo. Except that people tend to toot their horn in anger at Volvo drivers. I was a bit late when the light changed to red in heavy traffic and I was blasted by some fat-ass ponce in a Mack truck. I stopped my Volvo and got out, holding up all the traffic, and walked back to the truck.

'Did you want something, mate?' I asked, quite politely.

The trucker said in a timid voice, 'The lights have changed.'

'Gee,' I said, 'so they have, and your lights will change too if you blow your horn at me again.' Had he wanted to continue our little discussion, the next light he would have seen was the one on top of the ambulance.

The trucker's name, address and phone number was written on the door, so I pulled out my pen and notebook. The trucker didn't like this. I said to him, 'Listen, sport, if you want a little road rage, let me know. I'm like a dial-a-pizza: I do home deliveries.'

By this time, the green light had gone back to red and I went and sat back in my Volvo. No one tooted their horn at me.

Sometimes it's good being Chopper Read.

The law does not allow me to hit anyone but I'm allowed to defend myself if attacked. Even at 46, I would enjoy the odd attack now and again just to see if my legal right to self-defence is still holding up. Fist-fighting killers isn't easy, as they are trying to murder you. Fist-fighting so-called tough guys is child's play because they will not put their life on the line.

But the fact is, I rarely get in any fights these days. I read somewhere that the great Leigh Matthews didn't play any social footy after he retired from the AFL. I am a bit the same. I played in the big league and there is no buzz in running around in the minors, so I mostly try to smile my way out of trouble, turn the other cheek and walk away. But, now and then, I still enjoy a good punch-up, providing that the other party won't run to the police if he loses.

I've stopped all medication. Sometimes I feel as if I'm going to lose my mind totally. I don't think a human being ever quite recovers from 23 years in prison. Everyone talks about Vietnam veterans. Most of the Vietnam veterans I know spent approximately three years in the army and one or, at most, two years in Vietnam. I've met them in and out of jail, and I've seen them under the shower with not a fucking stab wound or bullet hole on any of them. Except for one chap, and that was because the police had shot him after he shot his local postman for blowing his whistle.

My dad never claimed war stress and he spent 24 years in the army and fought in three wars. But Vietnam? Everyone seemed to come back war stressed. Everyone suffers from mental and emotional stress. Everyone except a prison inmate.

Have you ever noticed that screws that work in a prison suffer stress? Every man and his dog in any form of public-service employment suffer from stress. Prison inmates are the only people who suffer from no known or medically recognised form of stress disorder. Even prison inmates don't really recognise it – why? Because both the inmate and society know that the inmate placed himself in that situation and, as a result, no complaint is or will be recognised, regardless of how much permanent mental and emotional damage is done.

I offer no excuse or reason or pardon-mes. I've my own self to blame for my own life and no one else but me. All I'm saying is what I didn't know when I was younger was that the human brain simply cannot take on the sheer weight of mental and emotional stress that it has to take on to survive that life. I have been damaged. The scars and the tattoos on the outside are easy to see but the scars on the inside are just as visible if you really look.

It's like holding on to a tightrope a mile high above the ground with one hand, with the weight of your whole life hanging around your feet trying to pull you down. The human heart screams, 'Let go, let go, you've had enough.' You can't take it any longer but the mind says, 'Hang on, hang on, don't let go,' and reality becomes a dream or, in the case of the seriously brain stressed, the dream becomes a permanent nightmare.

In keeping with the bullets and big tits theme of all my books, I would like to thank Miss Shelley Hamilton-Smith for providing me with the necessary inspiration for a starved imagination.

I've been given full permission to use the lovely Shelley's photos in my tenth book but I have been quietly warned about defamation. Perish the thought that I'd dare defame the character of such a fine example of Aussie womanhood. I'm too much of a gentleman for anything like that. Miss Hamilton-Smith is a professional dancer and photographic model. A ready, willing and eager young lass always prepared to answer the camera call when needed. I could if I wished launch forth with some lovely yarns relating to Shelley. Not that the lovely Miss Hamilton-Smith has ever been involved in any activity that would or could be described as embarrassing, sordid or against the law. In fact, some of the yarns I could tell would be about various high-ranking Tasmanian politicians and members of the public service and police force who have booked a dancer for a private function, birthday party or end-of-year Christmas do, retirement dinners and bucks nights.

I originally got to know Shelley because of her interest in motor cars – fast, hotted-up ones – and her love of driving them. She also has more than a passing interest in firearms. Yes, that's right, firearms. She might look like a blow-up Barbie Doll but she is quite the tomboy and can drive a truck, shoot a gun and use a chainsaw as well, if not better, than most men.

Despite her professional occupation, she has a strong sense of self-worth and moral fibre. In other words, she's not some low-life moll. People generally misunderstand the mental and emotional make-up of ladies in Shelley's profession. It is quite true that a lot of them are scatter-brained bimbo slags with the personal morals of an alley cat on heat and on speed, but Shelley contradicts this commonly held general opinion and has a personal strength of character that raises her above the norm.

She talks like a tow-truck driver, and sounds very blokey and unladylike and, while she earns her living in a very, very female manner, she spends her time off in male pursuits. In other words, when she's not getting her gear off she is one of the boys.

Quite a few blokes have learned to their public embarrassment not to push this particular stripper too far and it's a few of these yarns I'd love to tell. However, while Shelley herself would not object, I'd have to name the drunken politicians involved and they would most certainly sue. Or try to. There's always a chance they would change their minds.

So I will just thank Shelley and leave it at that and maybe later on hint at some unnamed dancer and some unnamed politician in some yarn. You can either believe or disbelieve it, but for now and for legal reasons I will leave the topic alone.

If this next story was true I could find myself in a great deal of legal trouble, so it will have to be a believe-it-or-not yarn that might or might not be true. It's about a hunting trip in a state I won't name involving five men and one woman.

The woman, an unnamed stripper, was driving the truck with an unnamed nightclub owner at her side and her boyfriend in the back. He was carrying a Ruger 77-44 magnum, a four-shot carbine with a stainless-steel barrel and action and a synthetic stock. The truck was fitted with two large spotlights for night hunting. The other truck carried a high-ranking off-duty policeman at the wheel and a high-ranking politician at his side and a no-eared man in the back armed with a .44 Winchester lever-action rifle.

The nightclub owner, the police officer and the stripper were carrying G36 Glock pistols given to them by the unnamed no-eared man. The politician was so drunk that he had lost the Ruger Super Redhawk .45-calibre revolver given to him in the bush. The unnamed politician was so blind drunk his only interest in the drunken spotlit night-time hunt was if he could get a little closer to the off-duty stripper.

After several dozen shots were fired, the two trucks pulled up and several ice-cold cool-bags were pulled out, full of ice and cans of beer. A barbecue fire was lit and a night under the stars was unfolding nicely.

The stripper vanished for a private moment to attend a call of nature. The politician also headed off in the other direction for a call of nature. About three minutes later, everyone heard a scream of anger from the young lady and a cry of pain from the politician. It seems that, while the young lass was taking a leak, squatting down, the politician approached her from behind with his dick out. Naturally she mistook the tap on her shoulder as her boyfriend wanting a bit under the stars. When she realised it was a case of mistaken identity, she responded with quick justice. When you are under stress, you sometimes clench your jaw in a second. This was not good for the pissed politician. She clamped down and he was in serious trouble.

Everyone thought that a Tasmanian Devil had bitten the politician in the night. He certainly didn't go out of his way to clear up this misapprehension when it came to explaining his strange injuries. Oops, sorry, I have given the name of the state away. What no one could understand was why the stripper was spitting out blood. Had she been trying to suck the poison out?

Needless to say, the night came to an abrupt halt with the nightclub owner, the policeman and the no-eared man trying to stop the stripper and her boyfriend from shooting the politician.

'How could you mistake that fat slob for me?' yelled the boyfriend. 'I guess you are going to tell me his dick's the same size as mine.'

'No,' yelled the stripper. 'It's fucking three times bigger. That's how I knew it wasn't you.'

Naturally, it took quite a lot of pragmatic politics and general mental, emotional and medical patching up to recover from that. But, as I said, it's a believe-it-or-not story and certainly nothing to do with me.

Another wild yarn was a politician's retirement dinner involving an unnamed stripper in an unnamed state. A senior public servant was retiring. He worked in a senior position for the government and the goodbye bash was being put on in the private function room at Parliament House. The stripper had been booked and smuggled in. The retiring senior public servant was sitting in a chair and had been handcuffed by an off-duty high-ranking police officer.

The stripper came in and did her thing. So far, the story isn't so hard to believe – until, that is, the stripper went into a room to get changed back into her street clothes. When she turned around, she saw a fat, drunken politician she had previously encountered on another unpleasant occasion. She decided to play along, allowing the politician to undress until he was down to only his socks and vest.

Then, with all her magic and with hands as quick as lightning, she went into the night with all the politician's clothes, leaving the embarrassed, drunken, fat slob naked. She dumped his clothes in a rubbish bin outside and went home. The politician was discovered by members of the retirement function tiptoeing down a Parliament House hallway with several copies of *Hansard* covering his nether region trying to make it to the car park.

Why he was heading for the car park was a mystery, as the stripper had also taken his wallet and car keys. But, as I've said before, it's a believe-it-or-not yarn that may or may not be true.

Would I tell a lie? You be the judge.

News that Eric Bana, Andrew Dominik, Michele Bennett and the *Chopper* movie have been nominated for 10 Australian Film Industry Awards has just reached me as I write this. At the same time, I was told that some bloke – no name given or remembered – had been shot dead in Melbourne. Police believe him to be the bloke who shot and killed my old friend Mad Charlie.

I made some phone calls to find out more details. Yes, some no-name bum that the police believed to be a big-deal gangster had been shot dead in Melbourne and, yes, they believed him to be the man who killed Mad Charlie.

'Can you find out his name?' I asked.

'Who gives a shit?' was the reply.

The modern-day police forces are about as much use as an ashtray on a motorbike. They look good standing still, but aren't a lot of help when things get going.

Needless to say, the phone call I made was to a police officer. I made a second call to an old criminal friend. 'What's wrong, Chopper? Are you running short of shit to write about?' he asked.

'Yes,' I replied. 'So much so that I'm almost at the point of publishing your full name and address.'

'Yeah, OK,' said my friend. 'You don't need to get snippy about it. The bloke who got whacked was a fucking nobody who the police think was a somebody and the fact that we are having this conversation proves that he never did Mad Charlie.'

'What was his name?' I asked.

'Ask your newspaper mates?' came the reply. 'They reckon they know so much.'

'Yeah,' I said, 'but they get all their info from the police.'

The laughter began. My friend knew that the police were getting all their info from people who worked several levels below my friend and they gave the police disinformation which the police were convinced was the truth.

Remember, the disinformation begins before the shooting starts, then it is followed up with more disinformation after the action. Talking to any media friends or contacts I may have was about as good as talking to the police. Only the police contacts I have would tell me it was only a theory or one possible line of enquiry or investigation. The media people would tell you that it was the truth.

If my criminal contacts dismissed it as a non-event murder, that was that. If it were of any importance, they would ring me first via my dad. I would need to ring them. If the police think the bloke who shot Mad Charlie has himself been shot, so be it. Who am I to argue with greater minds than my own? Fuck it all. What the hell do I know?

I'm supposed to talk to some bloke named Guido Hatzis on the radio tomorrow. He's some half-crazy fake Greek radio comic who loves to take the piss out of people.

I just hope Guido isn't related to anybody I've shot or had to hurt.

The list of Greeks I've come up against is almost as long as the list of Italians, not to mention the Turks. I'm no racist. I'll shoot anyone regardless of race, colour or creed.

My writing is constantly being interrupted with phone calls from the media. 'What are you doing these days?' is always one of the many questions.

'I'm trying to finish my tenth book,' I reply. What I don't say is that if you wombats stopped ringing me every bloody day I might be able to finish the bloody thing. But let's be honest, when they do ring it's a pest, but when they don't ring it's a worry. That's the business I'm in now, so I just have to cop it sweet.

One female reporter who I won't name is an arts writer for one of the big newspapers. I don't think she has ever written a nice word about me in her career, yet when we talk on the phone it's always the height of comic conversation. The media in Australia all seem to like me in private, yet feel that in the name of political correctness they have to follow the party line and bag me publicly.

The overseas and international media I've spoken to couldn't care less. They haven't been raised on a diet of Chopper Read stories over the past 26 years. I've talked to Australia media people who were hearing stories about me when they were doing media studies at school, so it's a bit hard for these people to be objective.

As much as they try to be fair, they know that their editors or publishers or radio or TV bosses all have a set opinion on Chopper Read and, in general, it's not a good opinion. It's only a rare few that have the guts to offer their own opinion uninfluenced by their masters. American authors can have criminal records as long as both their arms and the Aussie media will crawl up their bums for an interview. But the 'We hate Chopper Read Club' is an established firm in Australia and new chapters are growing all the time. I doubt that they will turn around and all start loving me tomorrow, no matter how many AFI nominations or awards the movie picks up.

Who was it who said that a prophet is never recognised in his own land? I am, in the immortal words of Kris Kristofferson, 'A poet and a picker, a prophet and a pusher, a pilgrim and a preacher and a problem when I'm stoned; I'm a walking contradiction, partly truth

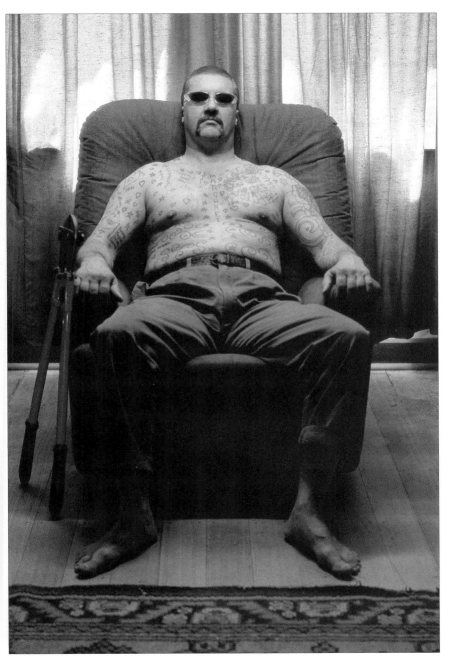

Armchair critic

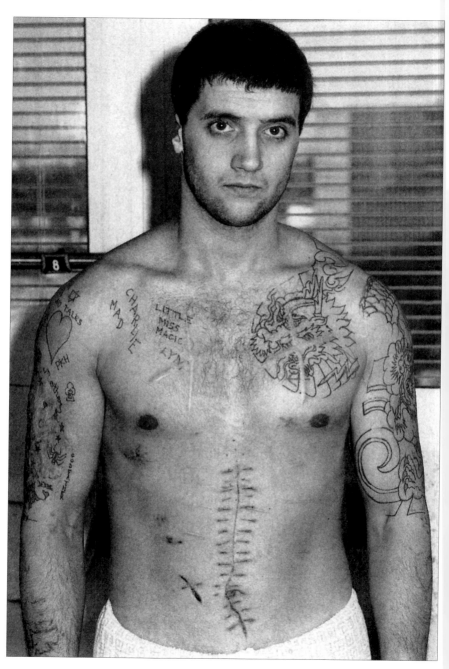

Spooky, isn't it? Me and Eric Bana ...

... but my scars are real.

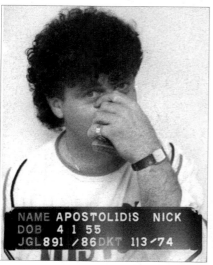 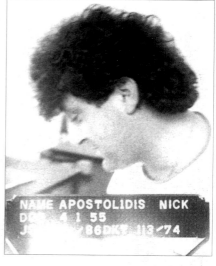

Two great actors. Vince Colosimo from *Chopper* (*top*) – his performance brought the house down – and Nick the Greek (*bottom*). I burnt *his* house down.

Who said I had an axe to grind?

Top: A great artist meets a bullshit artist. Suzanna Soul came to Tassie to paint me for the Archibald Prize.

Bottom: 'How big?' Suzie, don't be so rude.

Before I became politically correct, I'd have said bugger the Archibald, enter Suzie in a wet T-shirt competition.

The nips are getting bigger.

and partly fiction, taking every wrong direction on my lonely way back home.' Amen.

I've just got hold of the name of the Friday-night gangster who got himself shot, and who some police and media were trying to blame for offing Mad Charlie before his corpse was even cold. He was some no-name, would-be, make-believe Mafia punk named Dino DiBra. That's quite right, yes, yes, I know. I've never heard of him either. I think his only claim to fame was that he once waved at Larry Lambert from a distance of 300 yards and, as we all know, poor Larry only had a 250-yard claim to fame on Alphonse Gangitano.

So when blokes I've never heard of – 25-year-old punk puppies – are being held up in death as Mafia gangsters and no one's ever heard of them, I know it goes to show a gaping void of professional talent left alive in the Melbourne criminal world.

I stand corrected after another phone call, I must amend that remark, re gaping void of professional talent. We are forgetting the bloke who pulled the trigger several times on Dino DiBra – yes, the hit man. As always, the unsung hero whose name never seems to get a mention. The clue, as my friend on the phone said with a giggle, is 'Surf's up'.

I replied 'I thought you knocked those three wombats.'

'We did, we did,' came the comic retort. 'But they were not the only boys on the beach.'

As my friend hung up he was singing the old Beach Boys classic 'Let's Go Surfing Now'.

I'm getting too old for this shit, I thought to myself, as I went out the back to hang up baby Charlie's wet washing.

As I mentioned previously, I had to talk to this insulting bastard Guido Hatzis on Triple M radio. He called me Whopper instead of Chopper. I told him if I pulled my pants down he'd know why they called me Whopper. Guido Hatzis is a radio comedian, real name Tony. He is the master of personal abuse aimed at the unsuspecting. Quite funny, really. I've never shot a Greek I didn't like, so no offence was taken. Although I did burn Nick the Greek's house down ...

My life is entering the twilight zone. I meet people and they seem quite nice but within a short time they are into me for something or other. Pretty girls want me to put them in the movies. Ugly men want me to introduce them to the pretty girls so they can make their own private movies. Some men want me to kill their wives and some wives want me to kill their husbands. There are autograph hunters and head hunters who want me on their side. Then there are those who think I am rich and are looking for a quid.

It took me 30 years to become an overnight success. And, yep, that's the cue for my coach's address for success the Chopper way. Remember this, folks: everyone you want and whatever you want will walk towards you if you are willing and ready to meet it halfway.

But most people are only dream merchants, too lazy to take that first step. They wallow in a sea of jealousy and resentment because someone else of lesser importance and lesser ability reached the Promised Land before them. What they forget is that the other person had greater drive and a greater personal motivation. That's all it's about.

If you want to write a book, write one. Want to make a movie? Make one. Want to be a photo model? Get your photo taken a thousand times and haunt the magazines. Be an actor, bang on their fucking door till they have to open it and don't leave till you are dragged away, then return next day.

No glory without guts, as the old saying goes. Do you really think I would let Suzanne Soul the artist on to my place if she hadn't driven my publisher and myself mad? She wouldn't go away until she got what she wanted. In the end, that sort of grit has to be admired, not commended. If someone swims 100 miles through a sea of shit to climb aboard your boat, then, fine, they deserve a ride. But I'd toss a stowaway overboard.

Next topic, thank you. Maybe I should write a motivational book. I could call it 'Do Better, Or I'll Shoot You'. It would slay them.

My ongoing battle to have my firearm prohibition order lifted continues. I need a gun while working on the farm. Even Gandhi would want a shooter if he lived down here, what with the snakes and vermin. And now we have the fear that a fox has been smuggled into Tassie and is going to breed up. All right-thinking people should praise the Lord and pass the ammunition and eradicate the fox before the invasion starts.

Anyway, I continue to haunt Police Commissioner Richard McCreadie with requests that he reconsider the situation. His last two letters sent to me have given me some hope. Is he hinting that, if I took the matter to the Magistrates' Court, the whole thing could be reconsidered?

I will enclose the Police Commissioner's last two letters and let you be the judge. Chopper Read issued with a firearm permit. It will be a political hot potato and an otherwise small and normally short hearing before a magistrate would be turned into a media sideshow.

Politicians and police spokespersons would be asked to make comment. Any magistrate would feel pressured and I don't think I will apply this year.

But I will have to brief his immortal holiness Michael Hodgman QC and dispatch him to the Magistrates' Court in relation to this matter sooner or later. Chopper Read without a firearm permit – the whole thing is not only outrageous, it's downright un-Australian.

CHAPTER 7

FAME AT LAST

Thanks God I'm in top nick.

LET'S do lunch. I found myself sitting by the Hobart waterfront in the sunshine with my pain-in-the-neck, loud-mouth, larger-than-life, old-aged playboy, over-the-hill yuppie, millionaire-nightclub-owner mate Shane Farmer.

The Tasmanian premier Jim Bacon looked fried as he was doing some sort of TV interview not too far away. As our lunch ended, Farmer, as always, left me to pay the bill. As I counted out the cash, the media and TV people were getting set to interview Honey's husband. That's right, Jim Bacon's wife's name is Honey. Don't you love it? There are about a thousand different comic remarks one could make about any lady named Honey, but, if you add Bacon on the end of it, that number blows out to about two thousand. As Farmer and I walked towards the media people and the premier, we could hear the whispers: 'It's Chopper Read.'

The premier ducked to one side to get out of our way. I slapped him on the shoulder and said in a voice that could be well heard, 'You're a credit to the party, Jim.' He gave a nervous laugh and the media crews cracked up – or were on crack. I couldn't be sure. As I walked away, I said to Shane Farmer in a stage whisper that could be heard back in the mainland, 'How did he get into the ALP. We would have shot the wombat 20 years ago.' It was a joke, Jim.

Jim Bacon looks like a heavyweight on TV, yet when I put my

hand on his shoulder and felt the bone structure he definitely felt like a bantamweight to me. They say TV puts pounds on.

Thank God I'm in top nick.

We then headed off to Charles Touber's million-dollar, luxury beach-side, true-believer, ALP-to-his-bootstraps mansion and spoke deeply about the sad plight of the working class by the swimming pool. Need I say more? I don't think I should.

Just because you rooted a few gangsters doesn't mean you are one. Not a very nice saying, but true. One thing I can't cop is some wombat whose only credentials are that he or she knew or knows a few crooks writing books about crime and punishment.

My books are big in South Africa, but they're mad; a hit in New Zealand, but they're poor. I have been profiled in magazines and newspapers in France, America, Canada, South Africa and Bongo Congo. International fame at last. And well deserved too.

Michele Bennett is the unsung heroine of the movie. She's the girl with more guts than many crooks I know, who stuck with the project for years to produce the bloody thing. I hope she makes a big quid. I wish I could too, but then I can't get paid because I'm an old crook and they're not allowed to make money from anything but being brickies' labourers for rich folks, I guess.

Michele sent me a book called *Ronnie Kray – Sorted* by Kate Kray. As I read through this collection of old facts and so-called new facts – I would be the last to call anyone a liar – I came to her last sentence. It read like this: 'I have now started a new chapter in a new house and am busy writing a new book about the subject I know best. "Tough Guys" What else?'

I used to love the Kray twins, but, reading these penny-dreadful books put together by the various people who knew them, I'm starting to reconsider. I was shooting people in the legs at the age of 15. I carried out my first professional paid murder at 18 and, not to put too fine a point on it, after the third killing, Dave the Jew said to me, 'Well, Chop Chop, we beat the twins' record.' I don't think he was talking about the Bedsers. (They're twins who played cricket, you fool.)

I was 23 by then and it was five murders, not three, but the Kray brothers remained my heroes. It makes me almost vomit to read this latest Kray brothers crap. Thank goodness, I will be raising the literary standards of the old country. Shakespeare, Tennyson, Captain W E Johns and Chopper Read. Who would have thought?

I read a book and if I can pick out one thread then the whole book unravels as a collection of very clever, well-put-together stories which I accept are yarns and not facts. And I only stick to the facts in my books. Don't I?

I loved the Krays, not for their toughness or their brutality, which to me was little more than schoolyard nonsense. I loved them because they were the first crims outside America to adopt the Hollywood style of packaging. They took nothing and created an international English legend. To write yourself into the pages and fabric of a nation's history using little more than smoke and mirrors and bullshit is to be commended. They are the true and perfect example of the psychology of fear. They made other people believe they were dangerous using the psychology of fear.

Let's be honest, half the Kray firm was made up of semi-crooked businessmen and after-dark club owners and the other half was made up of psycho shirtlifters and between the bunch of them they whacked out about three men. They reigned for about 15 years and killed just three men. I've known card-carrying pacifists who have killed more.

Any gang running around Melbourne who only killed three men in approximately 15 years wouldn't get their names written on the back of a toilet door. So, yes, I do admire the Krays for their showmanship and their brilliant use of psychology to get legend status but I wish their wives, girlfriends and toilet cleaners would stop writing bloody books about them. It's starting to get quite depressing. What would they have been known as in Australia. The Yabbie Brothers?

David McMillan was one of the first major heroin traffickers to be arrested in Australia. Charismatic, young, confident and from a privileged background, McMillan was arrested in a 1981 joint police taskforce, codenamed Aries. He employed a former British SAS soldier to try to fly a helicopter into Pentridge as part of an escape plot. It sounded like a fantasy — until it was successfully done in Queensland years later.

McMillan was sentenced to 17 years in jail but was released in 1991 declaring he would make a fresh start. But two years later he was arrested in Thailand and again convicted of heroin trafficking. But McMillan always had money and dash. He was later to escape. His precise whereabouts are not known to the police, but there are people in Melbourne who are believed to speak to him regularly in the United Kingdom.

David McMillan was a yuppie millionaire bum. When I first knew him, we were both in the maximum-security Jika Jika Division in Pentridge back in the early 1980s. He fell out with Alex Tsakmakis and put a contract on his head.

Mad Alex, a millionaire himself, simply doubled the amount and McMillan found himself on protection along with his yuppie mate, Michael Sullivan. Alex Tsakmakis was not a man to be messed with and he could buy or sell McMillan and his mate Sullivan out of petty cash. Also, Tsakmakis was building himself a Pentridge power structure. However, it was rumoured that McMillan and Sullivan were bribing screws, even very senior ones. Their power structure was based on cash and they were willing to spend. Alex Tsakmakis was too cheap to pay a proper bribe. His idea of a bribe was to tell someone what he wanted and if it wasn't carried out he'd spend five, 10 or 20 grand getting their wife, sister or mother shot.

Sullivan could have represented Australia as a pole-vaulter. I couldn't see the purpose of the sport, although I myself would occasionally run around with a big stick. But, I digress.

Michael once asked the prison authorities for a pole so he could practise. Even they twigged when they found he could clear six metres, and some of the walls were about five metres. What he lacked in brains he made up in stupidity. McMillan and Sullivan were way out of their criminal depth tangling with the mad Greek but they did survive their sentence via bribes and corruption and being classed as high-risk protection prisoners. I promptly forgot them as non-events, not worthy of note, until people mentioned them to me recently, asking if I remembered anything about them.

My reaction was: 'What? Those bums? You want me to waste my time writing about those semi-faggot, la-di-dah, yuppie arsewipes?'

So here goes. (Get on with it. – Ed.)

When Dave the Dog got out of the Bangkok Hilton on a hot August night, to quote an old Neil Diamond song, no one had ever busted out of Klong Prem Prison in recent memory. This was 1996. McMillan, aged 40, was in a cell with four Thai inmates on the first floor of the joint. He used acid to weaken the bars, broke them, then squeezed his skinny half-junkie body through the bars and lowered himself to the ground using electrical flex. He got past the prison dining hall and a 'paid to sleep' guard, got a paid-for bamboo ladder, got over the wall and cut barbed wire with a cutter, also paid for and waiting for him.

He got through electrified cables unseen by any of the guards, undoubtedly paid to look the other way, and with a paid helper in the shadows ran to the canal and swam through a river of Klong Prem shit and vomit to a waiting car and vanished.

I have got no idea why Thailand is still poor after all the money they got out of Macca. His bribe money would have kept a small country afloat. You have to pay for cars, ladders, cutters and Old Spice to cover the smell of a dip in poo river.

All hell broke loose (shock, horror, he's gone!). Big deal. He remains the only Westerner to this day to escape from the 'Bangkok Hilton'. Or so the story goes.

I've heard other yarns that various UK criminals and American Mafia guys have been driven out of the prison to the airport and had all their paper work destroyed for US$20,000 cash which, in Bangkok, is a King's Ransom. It would go all right in Tassie, I've got to tell you. So I don't place much faith in the yarn that McMillan won when other men lost. Klong Prem is a turnstile, cash prison, meaning if you don't have the cash you rot or die, but if you have the cash and it goes into the hands of the right police and military personnel you are on your way.

For 20 to 25 grand you will get a ride home (with any luck you get frequent fliers with that) – or a bullet in the head on the way to the airport, after the escape cash has been handed over. The smart idea is to place five grand in hand and 15 grand after the police and military clear you through the airport – which, of course, would cost another few grand to sweeten the airport police and military personnel. They are separate units with their own bribe ideas. That includes GST (Greedy, Slippery Thais).

I don't know about you but I'm bored already. I'd rather talk about the little Greek babe Katerina and her asking me with a wink, 'How come all the good-looking guys are married?' I have the funny feeling that Miss 160 IQ Katerina was playing me like a fine violin. I would have preferred she played the pink oboe.

Anyway, back to McMillan. Yes, I know, bugger McMillan, and let's hear more about the little Greek head spinner, but this is a crime book and I have an obligation to include these shit heads. (Mark, please get your mind out of the gutter and back on the job, or should that be get your mind back in the gutter and out of the job? – Ed.)

Caulfield Grammar has punched out its fair share of freaks, such as the late Christopher Skase and that singer Nick Cave, and then there is David Peter McMillan. Like Skase (before he carked it), he is no longer in Australia. Or, like Nick Cave, he may be no longer on the planet Earth.

He faces three years' jail time in Australia and the death sentence in Thailand if he is ever caught. But he's gone. McMillan was a dreamer and a schemer with a restless creative spirit drawn to the dark side. He loved fast money and drugs. He was smart, ambitious and a heroin user.

He was in his early twenties when he got in on the ground floor of heroin dealing. He was a gifted photographer, cameraman and writer with enough contacts in the Melbourne television industry to do well. But heroin got him where he wanted to get to quicker. He was a good talker and even got involved in gemstone smuggling. What's the use of having a bum like a bucket if you can't jam a half-pound of heroin up it and a small bag of uncut gems. No doubt about those old Caulfield Grammar boys.

I guess you can't spend the last three years at school being humped up the clacker by half the footy team and most of the cricket team without using a somewhat stretched bum to some good advantage. I won't bore you with this wombat's legal hassles. If my publishers wish to include a footnote they can. (What, us work? No way. – Ed.)

Anyway, McMillan left Caulfield Grammar to go to Prahran High or the other way around. Mad Charlie went to Prahran High and lived in Caulfield. Mad Charlie was a lot younger but could still punch the guts out of every kid in the school. I don't know the details but McMillan always claimed to know Mad Charlie and Mad Charlie always said, 'Yeah, that yuppie poof, you watch him. He's on his way to a million bucks.'

I said, 'So what?'

Mad Charlie continued talking. I should have known he had a plan. He may have been mad and but he wasn't silly. That's why he wasn't called Silly Charlie. But I digress.

Charlie said, 'When he's rich, we'll have a million bucks and a dead fag in the boot of the car.'

It didn't happen. Macca is alive and Mad Charlie is dead so I suppose the pansy wins. And they say there is justice in the world. I would rather have one Mad Charlie by my side than 10 drug-rich, la-di-dah types.

McMillan only worried about looking after himself. His girlfriend died in a fire at Fairlea Women's Prison, and her family never forgave him. He got away. Good luck to him. If I saw him I would probably punch him and take 10 grand for old time's sake.

Yeah, he had charm, wit and style and he was a good-looking bugger to boot and he had a sense of humour. He had glamour. He was a posh wide boy. He was born a liar which means that fact and fiction didn't matter, it was the story that counted. He created his own myth in 1973. He vanished from Caulfield Grammar and ended up at Taylor's College and, quoting his friendship with a then 16-year-old Mad Charlie, became friendly with a former Marcellin College boy named Alphonse Gangitano who, as we all know, like Mad Charlie himself, was later shot to death by some unnamed party who used to be a mate.

McMillan was never going to be a tough guy or a gunman. He was pure midnight-express brains and polish, James Bond 006. Licensed to thrill, not kill, and drugs was where it was at.

Genius or not, his problem was the same as a lot of other moron crooks. When he kicked a goal, he couldn't help flashing it about. No matter how much money he made, he tried like mad to spend it, which is a dead giveaway. He spent and spent – on houses, cars and expensive toys of every sort. Even wealthy people started to smell a rat and a cunning old former policeman who lived next door down near Brighton somewhere smelled more than a rat. He smelled a heroin dealer.

McMillan demanded that anyone working for him should maintain a low profile yet he himself lived the life of the rich and famous. No expense was ever spared.

McMillan's girlfriend, Clelia Vigano, was one of the beautiful daughters of a hotelier and restaurateur called Ferdie Vigano. Clelia's grandfather, Mario Vigano, had married a European countess and was the proprietor of the original Mario's restaurant in Exhibition Street, Melbourne. A very posh establishment in its day. The family and the restaurant were both Melbourne institutions. I didn't eat there. Perhaps it was because I didn't wear a tie. It would have nothing to do with my lack of ears and my fetching tattoos. That would be discrimination.

Clelia was attracted by dangerous men, bad boys, but with McMillan all she got was a heroin needle. The lifestyle they shared cost McMillan years in prison and Clelia her life.

By 1979, McMillan had teamed up with Micky or Michael Sullivan, another looks good, feels good, talks good loser with a heroin habit. Sullivan couldn't fight his way out of the ladies' toilet, no matter how good a pole-vaulter he was.

Together they were a pair of snobs. Arrogant, paranoid shits.

HALF EDUCATED CHOPPER
"PROPHET AND POPE"
LIKES TO BURN DOWN THEIR HOUSES
AND RIP OFF THEIR DOPE
GOOD BLOKE THIS CHOPPER
NO BRAINS AND NO EARS
LIKES TO MIX WITH THE COPPERS
BUYING THEIR BEERS
ILLITERATE CHOPPER
"POET AND TOFF"
AN INCREDIBLE SHITMAN
WE'LL BE GLAD WHEN HE'S OFF
IMBECILE CHOPPER
"VERMIN AND PEST"
YOU'LL NEED MORE THAN A .410
AND A BULLET PROOF VEST
A HALFWIT OUR CHOPPER
HIS MEMOIRS YOU SEE
SHOW HE'S A MORON
WITH A HEART LIKE A PEA
POOR DELUDED CHOPPER
WILL NEVER HAVE ANY CLASS
LIVING IN A FANTASY WORLD
AND TAKING IT IN THE ARSE
HE THINKS HE'S A HERO
AND TO ME THAT'S A PUZZLE
'CAUSE THE ONLY THINGS MISSING
ARE A COLLAR AND MUZZLE.

JASON MORAN

I don't know if Jason wrote this, but if you're so tough how come the bloke who whacked your brother is still alive? Writing nasty letters to me won't get the job done. Continue with the poetry, you have talent. Love, Chopper.

CHAPTER 8

THE BRAIN DRAIN

I never let them lick me again.

THE shot passed through his open mouth, then, for some reason, did a sharp left through his ear hole and – just my luck – I was standing to the prick's left side. I had brain fluid, blood and a sort of yellow red stuff all over my neck. The .22-calibre magnum slug had spun past my neck. The body slumped to the dirt floor of the garage.

'Fucking hell,' I said. I don't like to swear but I was quite cross. 'Nice one, toss the fucking maggot in the back – no, not the Fairlane, the truck. I'll cover him in garbage and wood. We'll drive him up to the tip. Jesus, who told you to shoot the fucking idiot? Bloody hell. You get given a gun for 30 seconds and in a playful moment you shoot your so-called best mate.'

The trigger man (no names mentioned) was in tears and a total state of nervous breakdown. The victim, whose $150,000 Mercedes was parked out front, had to be dumped somewhere. I loaded up the truck. One of my dogs had already nuzzled his nose into the left ear hole and dragged out a good length of human brain and was proceeding to eat it. Sounds offal, I know. A hollow point .22 magnum slug goes in like a pea and comes out like a fucking watermelon. It was 10.30 at night. I didn't need this shit. I wanted to watch the late news, not be on it.

Also, it was raining and the window wipers on my old Ford truck didn't work. Great, what a drive.

We drove through the rain. I didn't know it but both my dogs had taken a flying run at the truck and landed in the back. You can imagine what had happened by the time we got to the tip. Let's just say that he didn't have many brains to start with, but even less by the time it came to rest him in peace. Or should that be pieces?

We burned the remains and his Mercedes, then, using the Council bulldozer, tipped the burning lot into the garbage hole which was the size of a small footy field. We then used the remainder of the jerry can of petrol we had to set fire to a giant pile of old tyres after bulldozing them in on top. It must have worked because we haven't heard a word since.

They later bulldozed the site over and opened a new tip so I won't tell you where, who, when or what but it was a dead-set fucking mess. That is a lesson for you. Never play with guns when you're pissed. I had to hose the dogs down when I got home after dropping my gun-happy mate home. They were covered in blood and stank. I never let them lick me again.

Accidents will happen and, once the gun goes bang, it's all hands to the pump. No time to waste. As I've said before, whacking the bums out is easy, getting rid of the bodies is the headache. Believe me, it is hard work.

Now on to Shane the Rooster. Now here's a yarn you won't believe. (What? – Ed.) This rooster was dead set like something out of the twilight zone. Shane the Rooster was named after my mate Shane Ronald Farmer. Both like to preen themselves and like to think they rule the roost.

Shane Ronald was a pure-bred Sussex Rooster, free range and wild. His size and ability to fight and stay alive was quite unique. He had three shots put into him with a high-powered .177 air rifle at close range, but it didn't worry him. He sat in the pine trees for two days and nights to recover then he had three rounds from a pump-action .22-calibre rifle put into him at close range and, again covered in blood, took to the trees and returned several days later none the worse.

He had so many bullet wounds he looked like someone who had been arrested by the armed robbery squad. His bloodlust was never satisfied. I found him covered in blood from fights with Wayne and Dwayne, his two rivals on the farm.

Shane was attacked several times by both my cats, Poop Foot and Ernie, and fought them off. Then Little Bill, my trusty Jack Russell terrier, had various battles with the big rooster. But, bleeding and near death, Shane fought like mad then took to the trees. Little Bill and Patsy Cline, my other dog (whose breed is still a mystery – a mix of Dingo, German Shepherd, Staffy, Blue Heeler and possibly Wolverine), started ganging up on Shane. But Shane always got away, covered in blood and half-dead but alive enough to return another day.

But one morning I opened the dogs' cage to let them out and they had not eaten all their ham, liver, kidneys, shanks and meaty bites, and, naturally, Shane snuck in to the open pen to have a peck at the dogs' dinner.

This time, Little Bill and Patsy 'Crime' were waiting and in they went. It was an old-fashioned doggy ambush. One had the tail, the other had the head but the big rooster fought and flapped and squawked so much that the dogs let go several times. I watched as the battle progressed out of the pen and into the yard and, in the name of Christian kindness, I broke up the fight. Shane was an inch from death, so I jumped on his head several times. I was wearing gum boots.

Later that day, I picked up the mortal remains of Shane and tossed him in the back of my truck.

The saga of the rooster who wouldn't die was over. Oh yes, I forgot, he had previously survived a blast from a .410 shotgun at seven metres, killing several unwanted fowl and wounding Shane badly. As you remember, I have no firearm licence, so I would have no idea what scallywag was shooting at my rooster.

Personally, I was sad to see the last of this hard-case rooster.

The next day, while I was about to load up the rubbish to take to the tip, I looked in the back of the truck and there was Shane standing up with a crushed head looking at me with one good eye. He was ready to go again. I let the dogs out and grabbed Shane.

'OK, big fella, rock and roll,' I said, and he did.

He nearly blinded Little Bill and cut Patsy badly with spurs as long and as thick as a man's thumb and sharp. Shane was a prize-winning rooster, a giant. I guess he weighed as much as a small dog and he stood over two feet in height.

A fighting cock would have had no chance in free-range barnyard combat with a monster such as this. I don't fight roosters in pits, but if they happen to have a blue in a free-range environment I let them sort it out the natural way. I'm a softie at heart.

I'm trying not to offend the Greenies and animal lovers but Shane was raised on grain and mincemeat, blood, offal, liver, ham and dead possums. He loved blood and he loved fighting and he had no fear whatsoever of dogs or cats or humans. He would have fought an elephant but we don't get many in country Tassie. They're nearly as rare as foxes. If you turned your back on this rooster for 10 seconds he would fly at you. He was just a mean, angry bird.

Anyway, the dogs got on top and I took poor Shane with a load of rubbish to the tip and, when I tossed my bags of rubbish in, I reached in to grab Shane and he sliced my hand with his spur then pecked me. He was still alive. This was starting to get spooky.

I tossed him in and covered him with rubbish bags and drove to the Campania Tavern for a few beers. I told no one the story. Who would ever believe me and who tells wild yarns about poultry that won't die? How embarrassing for a known killer like me to be unable to finish off a glorified chicken dinner. There is room for only one psychopath in my family. Shane had to go.

I'm left to wonder if Shane ever made it out of the tip and is right now roaming around Brown's Mountain. I feel a slight unease about the rooster who wouldn't die. Perhaps he will come back and peck me to death. Instead of a southern Italian, it will be a Sussex rooster which finally finishes me off.

To Shane, I salute you. In the world of fighting cocks, your name will be remembered and your legend will live for as long as people read this story and retell the yarn. *Via Con Dios, Amigo.*

Stuart 'Noddy' Attwood is his name. I've probably spelled Stuart wrong, which will piss him off no end. A retired gentleman such as myself must number among his friends at least one strip-club owner, being Shane Farmer; one nightclub owner, being Charles 'Charlie T' Touber – or 'The Dutchman' behind his back; one gun dealer, whose name need not be mentioned here; and at least one used-car dealer. And that is Noddy Attwood. A Tasmanian used-car king – sort of a Port Arthur Daley, if you know wot I mean, guv. You see, Noddy is originally a South London lad who migrated to Australia. So far he has sold me a Volvo 240 GL and a Mercedes Benz 280 SEL. The Merc is an old limo. All I need is a few Jews in the boot and I'd feel like a member of the fucking Nazi Party. I cracked this joke in front of his mum and dad, lovely people, but I didn't know his mother's granny was Jewish. I should have been warned. It's social death to crack the wrong jokes in the right company.

I seem to be constantly buying and selling cars through Argyle Quality Cars, Noddy's car yard. Shane Farmer, who dabbles in cars as a side line, is pissed off every time. Whenever I get rid of one for another, Shane screams, 'Go through me, go through me.' What he means is buy a car through him.

'I gave you that Toyota at a loss and you traded it on a Merc. Noddy ripped you on the Falcon and the Fairlane and you ended up with some shit-heap Volvo,' he said to me one day. He was frothing.

This nonsense goes on all the time. If I wanted a bulletproof Cadillac, Noddy could get me one. I love the comic banter of the used-car dealers. A nice collection of smiling rogues and scallywags. How come I did all the jail time and they get all the cash? I wind somebody's nose with a pair of pliers and I get jail time but they wind back speedos and it's called business. Perhaps I should have concentrated on car dealers rather than drug dealers. You work it out. My brain hurts.

But if you are in the clique you can get a good deal. I made Noddy a share holder in my movie venture, so, as a semi-silent partner (there is no such thing as a used-car dealer who can shut up), it's hard for him to say no.

I no longer mix with violent criminals but I don't mind club owners, pub owners, car dealers, gun dealers and the like. What the English call wide boys – not evil men but definitely after-dark bandits, to put it politely. It's a bit hard for me after a lifetime dealing with crooks, gangsters and hard men to start mixing with total square-heads, and blokes like Noddy, Shane and Charlie are as close to the edge as I can get and yet still mix with supposedly 'honest' people.

Charles Touber is a decent family man and a man with a good heart and a kind nature and, all sarcastic and tongue-in-cheek millionaire ALP yuppie remarks aside, he is a good bloke and undeserving of the comic pretend slander I have heaped on him.

It is just that these men are contradictions. Their social standing, political standing, public life, business life and private life all contradict each other. That is why I find them of literary interest.

Whatever they may or may not be, they are not boring. Charles Touber holidays in Cuba and, I'm told, has met Fidel Castro. Fidel probably had to go into therapy after the meeting – and count his fingers after shaking hands with Charlie. Or at least his cigars. Shane Farmer holidays in America and Thailand, and numbers among his friends persons he would rather I didn't name. Probably to protect *them* rather than him. Noddy holidays in London and, although a man who prides himself on his normal, everyday honesty, he attended the funeral of the late Violet Kray, mother of Ronnie and Reggie. I've noticed that everyone has a story to tell. My gun-dealer friend trains top sports people, but I digress.

'Why Cuba?' I asked Charles once.

'Because it's like stepping back into the 1950s,' he told me.

I felt like pointing out that we lived in Tassie, which meant we weren't exactly up with the Jetsons on the edge of modern living.

Charles told me other yarns which even I wouldn't write down for fear of my honesty being called in to question.

Michael Hodgman, QC, had met the Queen of England; my wife went to dinner with Princess Anne. Everyone has something of interest to tell you and, for a writer, it's hard not to betray a confidence. It's almost impossible, but I do try. Suffice to say Shane, Charles and Noddy are interesting fellows to talk to.

My mate Dave Lornie, the editor of *100% Home Girls* magazine, is going to Spain to visit his dad. I didn't know his dad lived in Spain. I've always dreamed of a holiday in Spain on the Costa Del Blanco or the Costa Del whatever. Who knows where my future may take me? Certainly not to Thailand or America with Shane – not unless I went to Reno to visit Sam Risovich. Not to Cuba with Charlie T, either. I'd probably go to London with Noddy provided he paid, but Noddy has deep pockets and very short arms. But Spain, yes, I can see that. Maybe when Charlie is a bit older – no, not Charlie Touber, my son Charlie, Charles Vincent Read. I can see myself in the sunshine of Spain and if anyone deserves a holiday

I do. I'm thinking out loud. All I can do is see where life takes me and enjoy the ride.

It is my great regret that I have not travelled overseas yet. Travel broadens the mind and mine was broadened by travelling from Pentridge to Geelong Prison. I was too busy fighting local battles to look overseas. A big trip for me was from Thomastown to South Yarra. I got jet-lagged going as far as Ballarat.

CHAPTER 9

SANDY

He had the backbone
of a squid.

BALDING, slight, with a sharp wit and an engaging personality, Alistair Farquhar MacRae hardly fits the image of a cold-blooded multiple murderer. But, according to police, he is probably Australia's most prolific killer, having been implicated in at least 20 suspicious deaths and disappearances and convicted of four murders in two states.

He was convicted in the Victoria Supreme Court of the murder of Albert Edwin Gerald O'Hara, whom he shot during a drug sting in Mildura. Police are convinced MacRae has killed nine people, and suspect that he could have been involved in up to 15 more deaths.

'I would have to say that he would be Australia's worst known multiple murderer and perhaps we will never know how many people he has killed,' says Paul Hollowood, who, as a senior Homicide Squad detective, spent many months investigating MacRae's crimes.

Alistair 'Sandy' MacRae made his name as a massage-parlour standover man, a briber of police, an informer and, last of all, a killer who thought of murder as a legitimate tool of his chosen trade.

Police still don't know how many bodies are buried at his 10-hectare property at Merbein, near Mildura, but he joked with friends that the small vineyard would never need fertiliser 'because there's plenty of blood and bone out there'.

Detectives have exhumed two bodies, and believe at least one other is buried there. They found the body of Domenic Marafiote buried under the chicken coop in 1987. Police allege MacRae shot and killed Marafiote on 18 July 1985. He lured the victim to the property on the promise of a marijuana deal but there would be no sale that day. Marafiote was a dead man when he accepted the bait. When he arrived at the property his grave had already been dug. Literally.

A Supreme Court jury was told that MacRae then drove to Adelaide where he killed Marafiote's parents, Carmelo, 69, and Rosa, 70. He was desperate to find the money that Marafiote was to use for the marijuana deal and believed the elderly couple controlled the purse strings. It is believed a large amount of cash was found sewn into Rosa's clothing.

Detectives say MacRae was so cold-blooded that before he buried Domenic Marafiote he repeatedly stabbed the body 'just for practice'.

MacRae was sentenced to a minimum of 18 years for the killing, and pleaded guilty to the Adelaide double murder.

He once told friends he had killed a woman, buried her on the property only to later exhume the remains, pulverise the bones in a concrete mixer and then pour the mix into a concrete garden roller, which has never been found.

MacRae moved to Mildura from Melbourne in 1983. He had been the second in charge to massage-parlour boss Geoffrey Lamb, who allegedly controlled a large slice of the illegal vice industry with the help of a group of corrupt police. But MacRae moved on after Lamb became addicted to heroin and began to lose control. Police say MacRae later chained the hopelessly addicted Lamb to a bungalow on the Mildura property in a bid to help his former boss beat the heroin problem.

In 1984 MacRae failed in a bid to establish a massage parlour in Mildura. He then met and befriended Albert O'Hara, who was planning to buy a houseboat-building business in the area. MacRae convinced 59-year-old O'Hara that he could make a quick profit from buying and selling marijuana. On 21 December 1984, O'Hara travelled to MacRae's property with $10,000 to buy drugs.

Police said MacRae shot him in the back of the head and buried him on the property. He then used oxy welding gear to cut up the dead man's car so it could be dropped, piece by piece, at the Merbein tip.

Flushed with his success after the O'Hara killing, he invited a massage-parlour contact, Johnny Selim, to visit him at the property in early 1985. He put forward a proposition that they form a local version of Murder Inc., luring people to the vineyard on the promise of buying marijuana, then killing them and keeping the money. Selim declined the offer and returned to Melbourne.

Police believe MacRae killed a rival underworld standover man, Michael Ebert, who was gunned down outside a Carlton brothel in April 1980. Ebert had bashed MacRae two weeks earlier and the beaten man had vowed revenge. The murder remains unsolved.

Police also suspect he killed his drug-addicted girlfriend, Deborah Joy Faher, 22, who was found dead of a drug overdose in a St Kilda motel in August 1981. Police believe MacRae may have given her near-pure heroin.

In July 1990, police found the remains of a woman buried in the backyard of a Kensington home that had once been owned by the mother of an underworld figure. Police believe the woman may have been an unidentified South Australian prostitute killed by MacRae.

In the early 1980s, police became concerned at the number of unexplained deaths of drug-addicted prostitutes who died from overdoses. A homicide taskforce investigated about 15 of the cases. The common denominator was that they all knew MacRae. He was extradited to Adelaide to stand trial on the Marafiote double murder. Faced with overwhelming evidence, he pleaded guilty.

The prosecutor said he should die in jail and said he should have a non-parole period of 40 to 50 years. 'This case comes into the worst category for several reasons,' Mr Paul Rofe, QC, said. 'On each occasion he has come before sentencing court, the words cold-blooded, planned and execution have been used. At the end of the day the public are certainly entitled to think this man should die in prison.'

When he was about to be sentenced, MacRae addressed the judge asking to be allowed to die in jail. 'To allow me leniency is a luxury I did not extend to my victims. The only way to show my remorse is to ask the court to show the same leniency that I showed my victims – absolutely none. I would ask the court to give me no possible chance of release before my death in custody.'

South Australian Supreme Court Judge Justice Williams gave him two life sentences and extended his non-parole period to 36 years. He could be released in 2023, aged 74.

The standover man made a career from identifying victims who were powerless. Like a jackal, he dwelled on the weak or the isolated. He tried to keep away from any criminals who had their own power base. But, when he targeted the Marafiotes, he showed he had not done his homework. The family was connected to a strong South Australian-based Mafia group who decided to reach out to MacRae before he was extradited to Adelaide. They knew he would be expecting a payback when he arrived in South Australia so they planned their move while he was still in his Melbourne prison.

MacRae was often protected in jail because he was to give evidence on police corruption. But Mark Brandon Read was known for his ability to find enemies inside – whether protected or not. Read was prepared to help organise the payback attack on MacRae for the crime family. His motive was hardly to right a wrong but rather to establish a debt of honour with the crime family.

Now in retirement, Read is still well connected with the Mafia in South Australia and can call in favours for more than homemade lasagna if he wishes.

'You can never have too many friends,' he says.

Sandy MacRae was a one-time prostitution and drug boss and, like others of his ilk, he was a dangerous man with a needle full of heroin or when attacking the unsuspecting, but, around real hard men, he had the backbone of a squid. He smelled a little like one as well. He ran a multi-million-dollar empire in Melbourne throughout the 1970s and 1980s and ended up with nothing he couldn't fit in a prison cell.

His claim to fame was that he murdered Rosa and Carmelo Marafiote in the 1980s. He liked to inflict pain but wasn't so keen on getting the favour returned. He was stabbed to near-death in a self-defence attack by Joe 'The Boss' Ditoria. Sometimes attack is the best form of defence, you know. Just ask George Bush. This attack elevated Joe 'The Boss' to the rank of underboss, bodyguard and right-hand man to South Australian Mafia Don Pauly A. I won't mention his last name. I'm sure he won't either.

The stabbing of MacRae was widely believed to be the direct result of tactical and strategic advice given to Ditoria by my good self. In a bizarre coincidence, I was the main witness for the defence that resulted in Ditoria's acquittal on the attempted murder charge relating to the MacRae attack.

My recollection was that crazy Sandy attacked poor Joe for no good reason and The Boss, a pacifist at heart, was forced to defend himself by stabbing MacRae until Sandy looked like a Vlado's steak, which is possibly an insult to the most excellent meat purveyed by a fine restaurant. Sorry, Mr Vlado.

Anyway, as a person of good repute, naturally enough, my version of events was accepted without hesitation and Joe's name was not tarnished by any scallywag suggestions that he attacked Sandy on the instructions of others.

Thank God for our justice system.

This is a footnote to a larger yarn and the lifelong debt that Joe 'The Boss' owes me. Via some members of the South Australian Italian clans, my source of Mafia information within Australia is second to none. I have been known to learn of a hit or a proposed hit six to twelve months before it happens. Good men remember how to repay a debt. I have a better forecast rate than the weather bureau. They get it wrong when they predict hail but I get it right when I say to don protective gear because a hail of bullets is on the way.

Enter Mr Jack Rennie, a boxing trainer of some note to those who have a memory, of 28 Marco Polo Street, Essendon. It came to my attention that a cousin of my old and dear friend Charlie M had been sent from Italy to carry out a pre-paid contract to kill Rennie. In 1991, Big Al Gangitano scuttled to Italy for a long holiday. Cynical scallywags suggested he scuttled off because I had got out of jail and he didn't want to run into me over a latte in Lygon Street. I would never suggest he ran away, but it was obvious he needed a holiday for his health and his nerves.

Any rate, Alphonse lost his temper in Italy and had arranged to have an Italian boxer trained by Rennie killed. Problem was that the Italian boxer was related to the Marafiote family and was the son-in-law of Pauly A. Alphonse was told that any hit on the young Italian would mean he would be hit right back, and would also die, so

Alphonse threw a hissy fit and decided to have Jack Rennie whacked out instead.

That's the way some in the underworld work. Al wanted to kill a boxer for some stupid reason and, when he was frightened out of that, he decided to kill the trainer. It is a matter of power and ego — and unbelievable stupidity. It's not *who* you kill, it's the fact that there must be a death to show one and all in the boxing world that when you ask for a favour you expect it to happen.

Alphonse was a sore loser, particularly when deals were supposed to be done. He didn't like being ignored and, when he paid $25,000 for the fight to be fixed, he expected the right result. Alphonse bet at 15 to 1 and lost the lot. He was not happy.

In short, Alphonse was out $25,000 and, more importantly, had lost face. Then he was told he couldn't kill who he wanted to kill, losing more face. He had paid US$10,000 to Charlie M's cousin, whose real name I now forget (and I certainly will not remember if any police are inclined to ask me), to come to Australia and kill Jack Rennie.

It would take years for the deal to be done. As it happened, the hit man arrived some months after Alphonse Gangitano himself was shot to death. I was then asked for moral and ethical advice. Should the hit on Rennie be carried out?

Cash had been taken, a solemn oath had been given, even though Alphonse was dead and, according to many, had even changed his mind and no longer wanted Rennie to die. The deal had been done, it couldn't be undone. Rennie was a dead man walking even though no one wanted it to happen. The hit was in place, the hit man was in Australia, and a good friend of mine — that I had once given evidence for — had provided him with a gun. It was all very complicated. The thinking, if you can call it that, was that a promise had been made and the late Gangitano had not formerly withdrawn the contract — as to do so would cost him another US$10,000 to compensate the hit man and his family for general inconvenience. It was all very Italian and highly complex. I was called.

'What do we do, Chopper?'

'Simple,' I said. 'Hit the hit man.'

'I can't,' came the reply. 'He is a guest in my home; the whole thing is insanity.'

'Well, what if he is put off by a non-Italian?'

There was a long silence. 'I don't know anything, we haven't spoken,' came the reply.

'Tell your Italian visitor to meet Dave the Jew at the Tower Hotel in Collingwood. Tell him Dave will drive him to Jack Rennie's gym, OK?'

'Yeah,' came the reply. 'After that, don't tell me no more.'

To cut a long story short, the young Italian hit man arrived and was never seen again. The Jew never went to the Tower Hotel but, to appease Charlie M for the death of his young cousin, I ordered the Jew to hit the guy who whacked the cousin. Everything had been paid off and out. This is all very Italian: honour and betrayal all rolled into one. Friends called on to kill friends, relatives called on to kill relatives. Do you think it's true? I'm not saying. I've got myself into too much legal hot water for swearing to the truth in stories, so believe it or not. Don't ask me to swear to anything, OK, because I don't want to end up giving evidence about obscure disappearing Italians and others. I will say, however, that this saga re the hit on Jack Rennie went from 1991 to early 1999 and all because Gangitano was too cheap to pay the US$10,000 consolation fee. You pay for a hit, you have to pay the same price to cancel it. And it's not tax deductible.

The arguments over this issue lasted nearly 10 years. Now, that is hard to believe and I don't expect everybody to believe it, which suits me fine. In fact, the fewer that believe it the better.

Anyway, this story is dedicated to the late Carmine Colosimo. Don't ask. You figure it out.

Reno, Nevada, is surrounded by desert, sand and more sand. A story told to me that I can either believe or disbelieve is about a Japanese 'Mafia' guy who won over a million dollars cash playing craps, as in dice. As everyone knows, the Japanese call their 'Mafia' the Yakuza … or is that singing in a bar when you're pissed?

The people he won the money from were doing business with the Japanese, however, a million cash is a million cash. The Japanese was driven to a private airport and went aboard his private jet with his million dollars and three blonde hookers he wanted to take back to Japan with him.

It was like a scene from the movie *Casino* starring Robert De Niro, Sharon Stone and Joe Pesci. The plane wouldn't start, so back to the hotel they went. The Japanese, his body guards, the three hookers and his million dollars. The boys who wanted the million bucks had electrified the penthouse spa bath knowing that the Japanese loved to tub up. They had the spa wired up while he was on his way to the airport. However, the handyman doing the job had hooked up enough voltage to cook the whole hotel. When the Jap and the three hookers got into the spa and one of the wise guys involved turned the power on from the basement, it blew the power in the whole hotel. It fried the Jap and the three hookers like boiled chicken and the boys got their million back, but they had to pay for a new fuse-box. And more.

The power to the hotel was on the fritz for several hours. It emptied the casino and cost the casino boss several million in lost earnings. In fact, the whole exercise cost the casino boss three to four million. They tossed the electrician out of the sixth floor of a nearby hotel because they couldn't take the lift up in their own because the power was off.

Sometimes, said the storyteller, it is just better to let the fuckers walk away because killing the arseholes can cause more trouble than the money is worth.

Two years later and they still can't get the smell out of the Penthouse. They say it was like a cross between chicken and fish which, of course, would be a little like crocodile. Yummy.

The thing was that the Jap and the three hookers boiled to death in electrified water for 20 minutes before every power panel in the whole casino blew. I suspect there would not be many worse sights than finding three hookers in a cooker with a Jap who's gone zap. It was, to use an American term, a goddamn nightmare.

To top if off, insurance wouldn't pay out and it cost over a million to fix the damage. In the old days, we would have just shot the Jap on the way to the airport but these days everyone wants to be so fucking hi-tech. All the hit men think they are James Bond 007. Instead of whacking a guy with a hammer over the head, they want to put battery acid in an ice cube and watch the guy choke to death at the table – or bomb his car using remote control and before he gets to his car some prick uses a mobile phone and the fucking car blows up 50 feet from where the guy is standing and kills a little old lady and three schoolgirls.

Call me old-fashioned. The highest technology I would use is a blow torch. Pain is pain, but, then again, I'm just an old-fashioned guy.

The hi-tech Mafia is gone, I'm glad to say. They have all gone back to the old stock-standard shot-in-the-skull routine. Killing people should be kept neat, clean and quick. No mess, no fuss and no complications. Electrified spa bath, indeed! They were lucky they didn't burn down the whole casino and, yeah, this is a believe-it-or-not story. What the hell do I care?

Excuse me while I go and have a bath.

The psychology of fear, as I've said, is a collection of dangerous lies and myths. All my life I looked up to the Kray brothers. One of the most famous yarns relating to the Kray twins was when Ronnie and Reggie visited New York and met with Mafia boss Crazy Joe Gallo. It has taken me 30 years to find out that when the twins visited New York they never met with any Mafia boss at all, let alone the great Crazy Joe Gallo.

Add it up, the twins had photos taken of nearly everyone they had ever met in their life and Gallo was an egomaniac. He loved his photo being taken, yet no photos of the twins meeting with Crazy Joe ever appeared. Because none was taken. By the time the story was told, Crazy Joe was dead, shot to death in a Mafia war, so the twins had no one to argue with them.

In my writing and ringing America to research this book, I found that the old story of the twins meeting with Crazy Joe and his brother Larry 'Kid Blast' Gallo was bullshit. The Gallo brothers were fighting a gang war at the time of the twins' visit and the twins' fame didn't reached America until after their arrest. To suggest that the Gallos would stop everything to meet with twin brothers they had never heard of was far-fetched. In conversation with American friends, this topic came up.

'Just say you came to America and met with Reno Garchi,' said Charlie the Yank. 'I mean, he died last year, but who will ever know?

Top: I work on a farm, she wears the torn jeans. Go figure.

Bottom: Honey, I shrunk Chopper.

Don't try the vindaloo. Art emulating life. A photo of me…

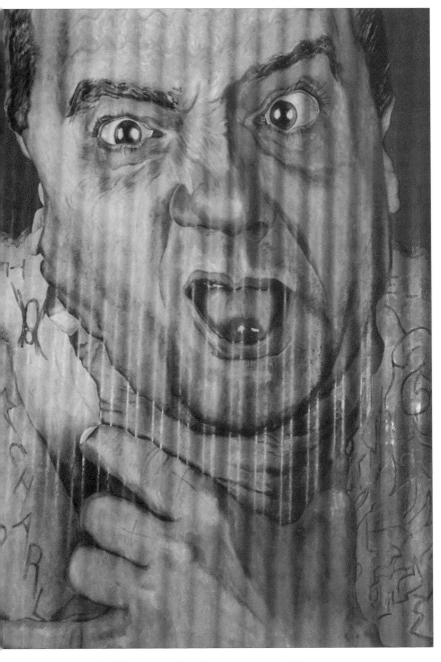

... and the Archibald entry painted on corrugated iron.

Three generations of the family ... me with my dad Keith and son Charlie.

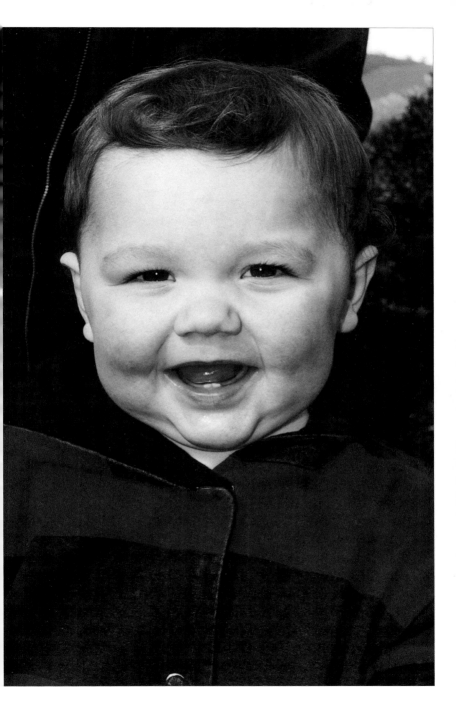

Mob connected? Surely not! In America you get locked up for *not* carrying a gun. Friends Sam and Dane.

I've always said tits and guns sell books. We're headed for the best-seller list with Shelley.

The grin reaper, taken by the world's best photographer, Chris Budgeon.

Them fucking Pommy twins pulled the same stunt in their book with Joey Gallo.'

'What?' I said. 'Ronnie and Reggie never met Crazy Joe Gallo?'

'I've never met the Queen of England,' said Charlie. 'But I've been to England and stood outside her house. I could always say I went to a garden party and met her. I mean, is she gonna argue? She wouldn't know who she's met and who she hasn't met. But I can tell you, Ronnie and Reggie never met the fucking Gallo brothers in their lives. But who's gonna bother arguing. After all, it's only a book.'

In a way I was sort of pleased that, like me, the legend of the Krays was a hundred facts and a thousand fairy-tales. There would be people who would swear they did things they didn't do and they would have got away with a million things and never been caught. Just like me. An enigma wrapped in a myth and then covered by a legend. Or in my case, a psychopath wrapped in an overcoat and wearing underpants.

It doesn't mean there isn't a hell of a lot of truth in amongst all the rubbish, it just means that as I grow older my heroes and the idols of my youth are becoming more human and less super-human. I always found the 'we met the Gallo brothers' yarn just a touch hard to believe. They had enough truth to tell but were yarn-spinners and couldn't resist giving the public leg a little pull. I don't condemn them for it, although it is not something a respected author like my good self would ever indulge in. Much.

Next topic. As I've mentioned, I've formed a small business venture with my dear friend Sam Risovich in Reno, Nevada, called 'Little Reno Films'. Who knows? I may be the next international Australian media mogul, although I am not as ruthless as the other one. And I'm a lot more lively than Christopher Skase.

Sam was telling me that once a year he visits Bill Gates and his uncle is Dr George 'The Jew' Rathman, the bio-tech king, and that in his younger days he used to take underworld boss and Mafia money man Meyer Lansky on fishing trips on some lake in Nevada. Fishing for cutthroat trout, I imagine. He told this to me in an off-hand manner. I was impressed.

I said 'Do you have a photo of Meyer Lansky?'

He told me that Meyer never liked his photo being taken but he did have a personally signed photo sent to him by Lansky in 1969. Sam is 52 years old. As a kid he would take Lansky fishing and place bets for him at the casino and the track. He was more a part of Lansky's friendly social set than his underworld set. This was hard to believe until Sam sent me a copy of the photo signed, sealed and delivered.

'No one can call themselves a made guy if they haven't met Meyer Lansky.' – Sam Risovich.

Of course, when Lansky died in 1979, this quote became a tad unfair, as Sam himself will agree, but the point I'm trying to make is that you shouldn't swallow everything in these supposedly completely factual two-bob gangster books that come out of England. Jesus, I hate big mouths who write outrageous things in books. It shouldn't be allowed.

In a recent letter to Mr Ray Wheatley, editor of Australia's biggest boxing magazine *Title Fight*, I felt the need to vent my spleen on the psychology of fear trick that is being used by the new spoiled-brat punk kid of boxing. I am talking, of course, about that Mummy's little boy and Daddy's pride and joy Anthony – the so-called 'Man' – Mundine. The kid who travels with his own brass band and who so far has fought the boxing world's version of toilet paper. As in half a dozen blokes who aren't boxers and then one who used to be – 10 years ago.

What more could you expect from a bum, to use that old boxing expression. I asked in the letter how I could get in on this comedy caper and asked, if I promised not to hurt the kid too much and take a dive in the third, would I be paid in cash, cheque or by credit card. I also quoted Mundine's hero Muhammad Ali in that all the hype in the world won't make a chimp into a champ – or a chop into a steak for that matter.

The tactics young Anthony and his camp are using is a classic example of the psychology of fear. He is setting about creating his own legend, his own reputation, his own myth, using a mixture of fact and fiction. The psychology of fear works best when fear and/or violence is a large part of the lifestyle you're involved in. Mundine is living proof that this tactic works. It's a lie but if enough people believe the lie then the lie becomes truth. Just watch him and see if I'm wrong. Until he runs into a real fighter who's trying. There'd be a dozen in Detroit or LA who could mince him.

As Sam says: 'No-one can call themselves a made guy if they haven't met Meyer Lansky.

CHAPTER 10

SHARK BAIT

I only hope you are alive when
this book hits the shops.

SURF'S up yet again. Out of the blue, one of the original thinkers I first wrote about sent me a photo of a young blond guy holding two semi-automatic handguns. I've had to blank out his face and have the photo redone so that his identity cannot be proved. It appears that a new boy has been found. He comes from the Gold Coast and is a former member of the Queensland Police Force and former army medic. A first-class CV for a psychopath. He has a firearm permit, loves surfing, has a passport and will carry out bang bang you're dead hits (and leaves them where they lie) for $15,000 a time. Cheap, really. Hasn't he heard of inflation?

His codename is Dominik, after Andrew Dominik, the director of the *Chopper* movie but he is nicknamed The Shark. He has been tested in Melbourne on a small no-name hit on a young punk Italian 'free of charge' before being recruited into the team.

I enclose the touched-up photo to prove that what I'm saying could very well be the truth. I cannot go too far as I don't want to involve myself in legal problems.

His first major hit was planned for a very well-known member of the old-school-tie underworld. I don't know why I was sent the photo but I will touch it up, copy the touched-up photo and destroy the original. I guess I'm the one keeping a record of these things and The Shark insisted the photo be sent to me with instructions to blank the face out. Which proves that, in spite of themselves, their massive egos know that I am the recorder of history — after it happens, as it happens and, spookily, before it happens. I feel just a little ill at ease as this could place me in legal hot water. I don't want to end up in court in more hot water than a hooker in an electrified spa, so I will add this disclaimer. This could all be bullshit and simply another part of the psychology of fear.

To Dominik 'The Shark', all I can say is everyone who has ever pulled the trigger for the original thinkers is now dead. You view yourself as a new breed but you're playing chess with the masters and I suspect you are only equipped to play draughts. I only hope you're still alive when this book hits the shops but, for some reason, I doubt it.

You have been recruited for one hit, one big hit only. You'll get your money then the surf won't be up for you no more. I doubt you'll even be alive to read this. However, if you prove me wrong, you could be the Beach Boy the original thinkers are looking for, as their list is far from finished.

I was once like you, Dominik, but I wasn't working for blokes like me. That's the difference.

May you live a long life but I very much doubt it. I suspect The Shark will end up as Flake.

A friendly tip, kid. Get rid of the big automatics. A .22 magnum revolver is all you need. I used to love autos but experience taught me that a sawn-off shotgun or a small calibre .22 handgun or a .32 calibre, or even a .38 revolver is best. Autos are just for blow and show. When it's time for go, get the old-fashioned revolver. They never jam, and you can always hit somebody in the head with them. Take care, Beach Boy.

Dominik 'The Shark' got off the plane at Hobart Airport. He arrived with one of the original thinkers just to meet me. Why? I'm out of all this now. Every time I try to get my life in order, a hand from the past tries to drag me back. What time does the next plane leave? About 1.30pm? Right, you two wombats are on it. 'But I thought you might want to meet "The Shark",' said one of the original unthinkers.

I whispered into the ear of the unnamed person who was talking to me. 'He'll be dead in a fucking year if he don't come up to scratch. I've met him, goodbye, piss off.'

'Ever since you had a movie made about you, you reckon you're

Mister Big,' said the unnamed party. 'As far as I'm concerned, you get no more info off us.'

The Shark took me to one side. 'Listen, Chopper. I grew up on stories about Chopper Read. As far as I'm concerned, it's a holy religious honour to meet you and if this maggot is pissing you off say the word and I'll whack him as soon as we return to Melbourne.'

He was trying to flip his controller, so I had to double flip with a twist. 'Remember Dessie Costello,' I said to the unnamed party, 'the young bloke here has just offered to pull the same stunt.'

The unnamed party, one of the original thinkers, smiled. 'I told you he was a good kid.'

'OK,' I said. 'He's all right but at 1.30 you're gone.'

'What do we do in the meantime?'

I sent them both off to the Men's Gallery. Do sharks like pussy? Silly question. Shelley was putting on a strip at midday. I told her to spin my two visitors out and she must have as they didn't leave until 5.30 that afternoon.

'By the way, Chopper,' said The Shark. 'I'm not as silly as your mate thinks I am. I'll feed you all the info you want. Just let me know when my new friends are ready or are going to stab me in the back.'

'Sweet,' I said.

What a life, what a world, I thought to myself. I'm so very, very, very glad I'm no longer part of it, other than writing about it. Even that has its risks. It could be an old crocodile against a young shark. I know who I would be backing. Not everyone who picks up a Chopper Read book is mentally well. I write for those people as well. Their money is as good as anyone's. I'm dancing inside the minds of the mentally unstable.

Are or were the Beach Boys real? What about Dominik 'The Shark', is he a reality or just a kid with blond hair photographed holding two automatic handguns? Was Sammy the Turk just a bad payer out of luck. Only time and history will judge that.

Or maybe time and history will never know the truth or be able to sort out the fact from the fiction. Who would have thought the World Trade Center in New York would collapse after crazy terrorists flew planes into it? That is a classic example of the psychology of fear. Real violence backed by rumour and panic.

When would the next attack come? What about poisoning the water? Maybe we will all die from anthrax. Maybe every Muslim is a terrorist. The world goes mad and we go to war not because of what has happened but what *might* happen. I fear the terrorist may have read my books to learn the real lessons of terror. Never let the enemy know what you will do. Inflate your power so they are on the defence. If they *believe* your power, then that power is real. When next you're told a story or you read a book, ask yourself this: If the Japanese and the Germans had won the war, do you think we would be reading about death camps and prisoners of war starving to death? I don't think so.

Losers in war are savages, and winners never raped women or killed prisoners. Funny that. Maybe it's because the winners get to write the history books. We simply believe that every man is as honest or as dishonest as we ourselves are and that every man is as good or as evil as we ourselves are. We think that every man plays the same game of public pretend that we ourselves play. None of us admits that we are one or the other or a bit of both. Every person wants the world to view him as he wants to be viewed, and that in itself is a lie. It all goes to make up basic human nature.

The psychology of fear is simply one part of the human condition that I've delved into. If fear is not popular why do we sit and watch horror movies? Why are we so morbidly fascinated with death and violence and fear? Why are my books bestsellers when they dwell on the dark side? Because the human being by nature is a violent, vicious, brutal being. That's why. We kill everything we touch in order to survive. You sit and snicker at my humble psychology – yet you read on because you know that from the pen of this particular madman comes the unholy truth that we are all born in the likeness of God and then grow into the likeness of the Devil.

Yes, folks. Luke Skywalker is a fiction. We are really all Darth Vader. Yes, I am quite mad and there is no law preventing the mentally ill from writing a book.

Thank the Lord and pay at the door.

127

Dominik 'The Shark' ... give up the automatics, son.

CHAPTER 11

JOHNNY RULES – NOT

I was wearing a fashionable over-coat and carrying a double-barrel, sawn-off shotgun.

JOHN Thomas Corral was once known in the underworld as 'The Basher'. Then he met Mark Brandon Read and became known as 'The Limper'. In 2001, Corral's fall to the bottom of the crime world was complete. He was found guilty of stealing six bottles of body lotion, two tubes of facial scrub and a packet of teabags

'The publicity that "Chopper" Read gets is sometimes just too much for my client,' his lawyer told the court.

'Just this morning, for example, Chopper was on Bert Newton (*Good Morning Australia*),' Mr Pickering told Melbourne Magistrates' Court. 'He's everywhere.'

Corral also stole hairspray and kitchen sponges during his crime spree. Corral, 48, of South Yarra, had pleaded guilty to shop theft and theft from a motor car. Magistrate Noel Purcell sentenced him to 14 days' jail, which he suspended for three months.

I first met Johnny Corral in 1971 in Pentridge. He was a year or so older than me and was a young up-and-coming hood with plenty of friends and general popularity. He was also attempting to carve himself some sort of reputation as a street fighter, gunman and general hard man. For some reason, he picked me out as an easy target. How did it end? Let me put it another way? Ever read any books by Johnny Corral? Ha ha.

For a young gangster in Melbourne to have a go at Chopper

Read in 1971 would be like a Jew having a go at Adolf Hitler in 1921. He may have felt good at the time but the clock was ticking. An alarm clock.

You see, I wasn't just trying to carve myself out any sort of reputation for this, that or the other. I fully intended becoming the most feared criminal figure in the 20th-century history of the whole Australian criminal world and that's all there fucking was to it. I aimed low and then got worse.

Years passed and by 1977 Johnny Corral had carved himself out a nice little reputation for himself. Meanwhile, I'd started the biggest gang war in the history of Pentridge Prison or for that matter any prison in Australian history. I was also in the middle of a gang war involving not only the Lygon Street Carlton Italians but the old Painters and Dockers as well. They were busy times for a young bloke.

Then I saw Johnny. He was in Fitzroy Street, St Kilda, early morning. He was wearing a powder-blue three-piece suit. He was standing in front of a hamburger shop with some hangers-on and a few whores. I was in a car with my crew, whose names I need not mention. I was wearing a very fashionable overcoat and carrying a double-barrel sawn-off shotgun. The rest of my crew all carried weapons, too, as you would.

Johnny Corral immediately recognised me. But he somehow forgot that I was the kid he had had a go at all those years before. Wanting to impress his small group with the fact that he knew me, he asked me for a ride home.

So Johnny and two of his mates jumped into our car with me and my two mates. We got to his place and I walked him to his front door. Then I pulled out the shotgun and held it to his head.

'What's going on, Chopper?' asked Johnny. He may have had a nice suit, but he wasn't quick on the uptake.

'You don't remember, do you?' I replied.

'Remember what?' he said.

'Remember this,' I said and, with that, I dropped the shotgun to his kneecap and went bang. I forget which leg, but it didn't really matter. I left the spent cartridge behind and my dad drove me back to collect it that night, abusing me all the way for my lackadaisical attitude. That's what dads are for. They want you to improve all the time and to do your homework properly. You might think they are nagging, but they really do care. Thanks, Dad.

Johnny stuck solid and didn't give me up, but enough other witnesses did and I got two years' jail. This sentence went in with the sentence I got for attempting to kidnap Judge Martin in the Melbourne County Court in 1978, January 26 – Australia Day. I was always a patriot.

My girlfriend at that time was an 18-year-old prostitute named Lindy. Her last name isn't important. She bumped into Johnny with his one good leg and he told her his sad story. As my so-called girlfriend, she felt sort of responsible and guilty in a strange way, so Lindy and Johnny saw quite a lot of each other … and not just his crook leg either. A little bit north of his knee, if you know what I mean. She visited me and told me all about it.

'If you plan to fuck everyone I've ever shot, Princess, you'll be a very busy girl,' I said.

'No, I don't plan to screw everyone you ever shot,' said Lindy. 'But I felt sorry for him. I just felt so sorry for the poor bastard. One minute he's standing in St Kilda like little Caesar and the next minute he's getting around the place like Jake the Peg with his missing leg.'

I never knew Lindy had a sense of humour. I laughed. I wasn't angry. You can't have a hooker for a girlfriend then complain when people start rooting her. She only worked as a pro for two years, then turned into a born-again Christian. Only I could turn a girl off the game and on to God.

Gee, I loved her at the time. Like the old Dean Martin song 'How many tears have I cried over you – a million and one or a million and two'. So I won't mention Lindy's last name. I know she is a mum now with a grown-up son (not mine, I'd like to add). In the two years she worked in the sex industry, she was a weapon. I think she screwed every friend I had at that time, including Mad Charlie on a prison visit. I think she even tried to pull the Jew on for size. But as the Jew would comically say, 'Women are a poor substitute for masturbation.' Ha ha ha.

Anyway, getting back to one-leg Johnny being shot by Chopper Read. It turned out to be a pretty good thing for him for a while, as

I ended up with a lot of enemies and all my enemies looked after Johnny. However, after all, or nearly all, of my enemies died (at least those with money), Johnny fell on hard times but I'm told he still pulls the 'feel sorry for me' trick.

'Chopper Read shot me' boo hoo hoo. And I'm told it still works. However, I'm also told that the modern-day hooker isn't too interested in handing out a freebie to one of my victims. The modern-day hooker would rather hand one out to me. That's progress and who am I to stand in the way of progress. Ha ha ha.

The old 'Please feel sorry for me, I got shot by Chopper Read' story should be set to music and turned into a song because Johnny isn't the only one to pull that stunt in court.

As I write this a Mister Hedley Gritter rang me in relation to my taking part in a Melbourne crime movie named *Trojan Warrior*. I note since then that Warwick Capper reckons he has been offered a part in *Trojan Warrior*, too, although the film people are denying it. No wonder they don't want us on the same set. After all, I nearly shot him in the leg as a favour to Gilbert Besanko at the footy one day.

Great game, footy. They check your bag for beer cans but you can walk in with a sawn-off shotgun and no one bats an eyelid.

I let my good nature get the better of me that day, but I can't guarantee that I will be able to restrain myself again if I see the bastard trying to act. He did enough bad acting in front of the goal square without wanting to get in front of a camera.

I can't get to the football regularly these days but I still take an interest. The West Coast Eagles were interested in pinching Daniel Chick from Hawthorn. My demented publisher asked me to intercede. I wrote a harmless note to the Eagles coach, Ken Judge, suggesting young Chick would be better suited staying at Hawthorn. I made sure the letter was delivered to his home address. Chicky ended up staying at Hawthorn. A wise decision all around, I would think.

I slipped into Melbourne to shoot the movie (not Capper) and it was a great experience. Every scallywag in Australia had some sort of a walk-on role. I was a natural, I must say. So many star performances in the witness box prepared me for an acting career. I didn't have too many lines but, having watched Eric Bana, I'm sure it will only be a matter of time before my name is up in lights. Sorry, it already is.

Maybe I will be strung up. Oops, I already have. I think you get the drift.

A company named Saatchi and Saatchi rang me about doing a 'Don't Drink and Drive' campaign. I did and it was released in NSW to the predictable media outrage. How dare they use Chopper Read, blah, blah, blah.

The hacks descended and wanted to know if I had been paid for the ad. I hadn't but they had to try and create the controversy. I couldn't care less. If it saves someone from getting pissed and killing someone, then that's great. I have a lot of faults but I've never been mean with money, and always a soft touch for charity.

I was asked to donate a signed book for the Queen's favourite charity for kids with cancer in Britain. I sent it with a note telling her I had spent 23 years as a guest of hers, in her various prisons, so it would be churlish to deny her request. I also dropped a hint that MBR wouldn't mind an MBE. You don't want to die wondering.

I have also been used as a model for some sunglasses. I should be rich but, let me tell you, I'm not.

My life is a never-ending surprise to me, so being told that old one-leg Johnny used my name to get out of the great teabag robbery of the year 2001 came as no great surprise. As I often say to the bartender, 'Please don't pass me any more nuts, I've had quite enough, thank you.' Ha, ha, ha.

Rhys Muldoon is a Sydney-based actor who got in touch with me after the AFI Awards. He is a happy-go-lucky sort of bloke. A bit of an Aussie knockabout, full of shit, but a lovable scallywag and very serious about his craft. I think.

Once he heard that I had something going with J Walter Thompson and Black Fly Sunglasses and a 'Don't Drink and Drive' campaign, as well as my being asked to take part in a movie by radio 3RRR legend Hedley Gritter, Rhys seemed to think I needed an agent or some sort of management. I said that, well, maybe an agent would be a good idea in case shit jumps up in the future that I can't handle.

The bloke went mad contacting agents and managers all over Sydney. Now these people all want to talk to me. But I'm someone that no agent or manager really knows what to do with. I'm in the too hard basket or too fucking mad bin. Then Rhys rang to say he contacted Harry M Miller. Jesus, the whole thing is getting too much for me. I've sold almost half a million books and had a movie made about my life and the nation's media have spent more time up my arse than they have up the pub, and all of a sudden I need an agent.

So far I've been getting ripped off quite nicely without an agent. (I heard that – Ed.) When I talk to these razzle-dazzle merchants, they haven't got the faintest idea how to handle me or what the hell to do with me.

But, and not to be unkind, Harry M Miller aside, all the rest of the snake-oil merchants appear to be unemployed and very busy trying to find work for semi-unemployed members of the entertainment industry.

'When in doubt, shoot everybody' is a good motto. The more I'm tempted away from what I know I can do towards what I know I can't do the more paranoid I become. The name Chopper Read is so big, people just imagine that there has to be money involved.

This is far from reality. I agreed to co-write a film script with Rhys. What do I have to lose? But I have spent my whole life in a world of lies and disinformation and I can smell spin-doctors and snake-oil salesmen a mile away.

In the old days, when a man said to me, here's the guns, here's the money, this is the target, I believed him. But when anyone said, I'll pay you so much after the job is done I knew I was talking to a bullshitter or a game player. The Australian entertainment industry has more dreamers, conmen, liars and coked-out empire builders in it than the criminal world. In fact, in the criminal world I dealt with a better class of person, and that's saying something.

Of course, none of this applies to Rhys. I'm sure his heart is in the right place. I don't want to become a freak, sideshow, novelty-value-only commodity within the so-called industry. Rhys and I will no doubt write our film script, but already I know I would get dizzy and spin out if I had to try and live in the world these people live in.

Yes, Rhys, we will do the things we spoke of but, for God's sake, mellow out.

Sydney people are all the same. If they aren't going at 100 miles per hour, they are generally dead. Anyway, that's what I think.

A wise man once said, Don't let your life get kidnapped by well-meaning madmen. I should know.

God bless America ... American friends with American toys.

EPILOGUE

I can state with true
honesty that I've led a foolish life,
a wasted life.

IT was the Australian film industry's night of nights. They all got dressed up in their best clothes and just couldn't wait to be seen – and that was just the cocaine dealers. The starlets went to the hairdressers, the dressmakers and the plastic surgeons. The blokes put on their tuxes and put socks in their undies so they looked like studs. They all practised their surprised looks in case they won. They rehearsed their speeches so they could say they hadn't prepared anything to say. Most of them now have tattoos and drug habits, yet they never do jail time. Work that out.

For months, I would skip to the letterbox hoping for an invitation to the night. I thought I could go as Eric Bana's date but they obviously forgot my address. For a while, I thought of going and impersonating Eric like he had done to me. Would they have noticed? Who knows.

I decided to watch it from home in Tassie. They put on their tailored suits. I put on my old tracksuit. They grazed on sushi. I watched the cattle graze and ate nine steamed dimmies. They snorted some crack and coke. I cracked a Bundy and Coke.

Still, it was a good night and I was happy that the crew from *Chopper* did well. So they bloody should have, they had a great subject to work with. Eric Bana won Best Actor, Simon Lyndon won Best Supporting Actor and 'Doctor Strangelove' Andrew Dominik won Best Director. Michele Bennett did not win Best Producer for the Best Movie. A pity, I thought she deserved it. They gave the Best Movie to the Barbie-doll film *Looking for a Bottle of Brandy* or some such forgettable stupid name. Who did she ever kill?

Fame today, forgotten tomorrow, unlike Chopper who will ride off into the Stanley Kubrick sunset of a clockwork orange. J Walter Thompson has just signed me up on behalf of their American client Black Fly Sunglasses to act as their Australian front man in a national publicity campaign. Black Fly is an out-there, on-the-edge, plenty-of-attitude brand name, however in signing me they may have entered the world of mental illness. Ha! Ha! Ha!

My life takes on so many twists and turns. It can roller-coaster from week to week. Another artist, Andrew Hopgood, wants to paint my portrait for the Moran Prize. I wonder if that is the Mark Moran Prize because if it is they are painting the wrong bloke.

Suddenly artists and advertising agencies seem to like me. Julian Knight the Hoddle Street massacre man still drops me a line from time to time, keeping me in touch with the Victoria prison system. As if I needed to be kept in touch.

This time he included a photo of himself holding a Chopper book. Me thinks someone is hinting that this would be a good photo to use in my next book. Hint taken, Julian. Dominik 'The Shark' sent me a recent photo of himself sitting next to a dead man. I destroyed it, as to blot out both faces would not conceal the fact that the man Dominik was sitting with was, in fact, dead. How dumb is he?

The photo simply read 'Surf's up!'

I received a similar snapshot sent by The Shark's predecessors after the 1997 murder of Italian businessman Angelo Romeo. I was in prison at the time and destroyed that photo as well. This want or need of some to send me hints and snapshots hoping that I will record history or hint that so-and-so could have or may have or is rumoured to have done this or that to so-and-so is overwhelming.

Some view me as the official recorder of names and events that would otherwise go unnoticed. I don't mind but I know that I am also used by some in psychology of fear and disinformation campaigns, hoping that I will hint at incorrect information given to me by people working on behalf of the true guilty party.

For example, the Angelo Romeo photo was sent to me by a person attempting to hint that Alphonse Gangitano did it or ordered it done. I knew it was a contract job involving big money players within the illegal abalone-poaching industry and about a thousand miles removed from the world of Alphonse Gangitano. I even traced the handwriting on the envelope down to a friend of Gangitano's who had sent me another disinformation letter several years before. I forget the chap's name now, as it was all so long ago.

This epilogue is included for the benefit of those readers left slightly puzzled by the content of this book and the message and or meaning within.

I've been so careful to blur fact − true real fact into the fog of fiction − that some readers will be left to wonder if it is a fact or a fiction book. First of all, it is a 100% fact book. Every true story is true and every lie is a lie. All I've done is to choose not to separate the truth from the fine-weave thread of lies I've run through the story, in the name of legal self-protection and to show you in my own way just how the psychology of fear and the creation of lies, myths and stories in the making of a legend or the building of a reputation and a personal or professional image is done.

There will be those readers who will condemn me for trying to bamboozle them and other readers who will thank me for putting into words something they themselves have long suspected.

As I've said before, it's only a book and not a greatly overpriced one. The reader can either believe or disbelieve or, if they are smart enough, possibly learn something. From time to time I have made predictions relating to how long other people have to live and, surprise, surprise, I've been right quite a few times.

The fact that I entered the valley of the shadow meant I was a fool to begin with. The fact that I survived to tell the tale simply proves the old Irish proverb that God protects fools and drunks.

Just because a fool is smart enough to survive doesn't make him any less of a fool, and with age and an ego fast fading I can state with true honesty that I've led a foolish life, a wasted life. I've salvaged the remainder of that foolish life with a pen in my hand and not a gun. But I can't look back on my former life with any real sense of pride or achievement. It was only when I put down the gun and took up the pen that my life turned around. In writing about my life and the people in it, I came to understand that some others might see my past as a blood-splattered painting of death and glory.

I am like 'The Fool on the Hill'. Yes, I got to the top, but at what insane cost? A cost I wouldn't wish to have to pay all over again. I regret nothing. I continue to say 'Je Ne Regrette Rien'. At the time I truly believed in that motto but deep inside how could anyone other than a fool really believe such a thing?

As I grow older and I look at my young son, I know I would lay down my life for him. I would not wish my life on him or for him to follow in my footsteps and it is when I see my son that I know I do regret my past.

I guess I'm saying that the madman who first wrote the words and the motto of the French Foreign Legion 'Je Ne Regrette Rien' has grown old enough, wise enough and less foolish and honest enough to now admit that I regret so much.

The *Chopper* movie has been all over the West End of London and throughout the UK. I've only one slight complaint. I think Vince Colosimo who played Neville Bartos in the movie was the forgotten star. I know Simon Lyndon won Best Supporting Actor at the AFI Awards, but personally I would have given Vince Colosimo my vote. He acted so very much like the type of people I really did enjoy shooting. No offence, Vince, but for what it's worth I think you did a fucking top job. I know that I'm not meant to mention the movie in my books but how can I help mentioning it.

Eric Bana will go on and on to bigger and better projects. You don't have to be a fortune-teller to predict that, but I'd keep my eye on Vince Colosimo, too.

Anyway, that's my prediction, for what it's worth. As for Eric Bana, what can I say? I can only repeat the old story about Elvis Presley entering an Elvis lookalike contest and coming third. Bana looked more like me in that movie than I did. Like I said to a local newspaper, had the role called for Eric to wear a dress he would have won Best Actress as well. That's how good an actor he is.

Speaking of fortunetelling and predictions, I feel I must mention the name of my one-time friend, later turned enemy, Nick 'The

Greek' Apostolidis and simply say that I have a very odd feeling that I will outlive him. In fact, I'm convinced. I won't put a time or a date to it, as I don't want the prediction to be used against me. Let's just say, in the immortal words of Dr Martin Luther King, I had a dream. And that dream is to outlive the Greek.

Let's just see if this prediction comes true. Who knows, I may be a fortune-teller or, in Nick's case, misfortune-teller. I do get these odd feelings from time to time about people and the next thing I know they are dead.

Quite spooky, really. But, as I've said, it's only a feeling. I may be quite wrong. Nick might outlive us all, but I doubt it, but for what it's worth I thought I'd mention it. Anyway, Nick, if you are reading this, you'll forgive me for not sending flowers.

Tick Tock Tick, is that a clock ticking or is it a Ding-Dong Ding of bells? I won't crack any distasteful jokes about Nick. I burned his house down once. I should have got an award. Don't ask for whom the bell tolls because, if I was to crack a comic remark, I'd have to say it tolls for you, my old cavalier *Via Con Dios, Greek*. I love a sunburned country.

Anyway, as epilogues go, I think I've written quite enough. It's time to don my highway-patrol Black Fly sunglasses and walk away. A small plug for my sponsor. I will leave you all with this small thought. All any writer has to do is to capture the imagination. The truth of his words is for the reader to believe or disbelieve, as long as the imagination has been captured for the length of this book. What you decide to believe is up to you. Just because I have done foolish things doesn't mean that I'm a fool and, as far as the content of this book is concerned, only a fool would swear to the truth of it. I'm happy enough to let the reader be the judge. Not guilty, I hope.

Mark Brandon Chopper Read

THE CALABRIAN CONTRACT

A very short story

There is no reason for this picture to be here, other than it will sell books.
Thanks, Shelley.

AUTHOR'S NOTE

THEY nailed Christ to the cross for telling lies – or was it for telling the truth? Millions upon millions have died during the past 2,000 years in more wars than can be counted, fighting over this very argument, and still we argue over the fact or fiction of it all. On that note, the author of this short yarn informs you that this is a work of total fiction, but always remembering that many a true word is spoken in jest.

The reader could be forgiven for suspecting that the tapestry of all fiction is held in place by threads of fact, and the sceptics among us believe that so-called fact is nothing but a patchwork quilt of fiction.

The arch enemy of all storytellers of the modern era is the lawyer – a strange being who, for the sheer sake of argument and the relentless search for profit, will look every truth in the face and see a lie, and will also seize upon each lie and attempt to strangle a truth from it.

Thus, every teller of tales must, for legal reasons, clearly state that his is a work of total fiction. This one included. Sort of.

'Before Elvis there was nothing.' – John Lennon

DEDICATION

This book is dedicated to:

Alphonse Gangitano
Mad Charlie Heygeljai
Vincenzo Mannella
Giuseppe 'Joe' Arena
Marco Medici
Mark Antony Moore
Joe Quadara
Dominic Marafiote
Tony Peluso
Alfonso Muratore
Francesco De Masi
Vinenzo Angilletta
Liboria Benvenuto
Francesco Benvenuto

'And the men who have vanished and to the
men who will – and, believe me, they will.'
MARK BRANDON READ

CHAPTER 1

THE DREAMS OF YOUNG MEN

They were mindless, violent thugs.

THE murder of Melbourne underworld identity Alphonse Gangitano in the laundry of his home in Templestowe on 16 January 1998 prompted me to write this. However, I stress that this is a yarn.

Mick and Al were big men – six foot and built like heavyweight boxers. Mick had once been a Victoria champion, but on his way to the Australian title realised that a heavy right cross couldn't overcome a glass jaw, so he gave the game away gracefully. However, he maintained his easy-going, gentle-natured, kindly manner, unlike his best friend Al, who had the attitude of a junkyard dog who'd been sniffing petrol.

The two shared a single dream – to pull the Italian crime families of Melbourne together and create what they both saw on American movies and television as 'the Mafia'. Yes, the Mafia in Australia. The fact that there was already a Mafia in Melbourne, a true Sicilian Mafia, didn't seem to enter the heads of these two Calabrian tough guys. Such are the childish dreams of young men – dreams of criminal glory, power and wealth. Such dreams are the product of pure fantasy. But men who are strong and determined enough can sometimes turn fantasy into reality.

Mick Conforte and Big Al Cologne were two such men. Like Walt Disney, they turned their dreams into reality and it made them both rich at the turnstile. Crime is no different to anything else. A man has a dream and will either achieve it or fail. The difference being that, with crime, to fail usually means to die trying. There are no golden parachutes, superannuation schemes or preferential share options for gunmen.

'Such is life,' as old Ned said.

> 'If you put all the magistrates and judges in this country nose to bum in one long line, I wonder if they would get a clearer view of their responsibilities?'
>
> – RONNIE BARKER

The time is early 1974. The place is Johnny's Green Room in the inner Melbourne suburb of Carlton. Johnny's is a gathering place for old-time Aussie crooks, knockabouts, street fighters, gunmen, prostitutes, molls, madmen and up-and-coming, would-be Mafia dreamboat kids who think they can live out their own *Godfather* movie in Melbourne, Australia.

Outwardly, it is a coffee bar and pool hall, but after dark it is a gathering point for the gutter trash and heavy-cash trash of Melbourne's supper-club criminal world. It was also the first time a 16-year-old schoolboy named Al Cologne, a posh Italian from a well-to-do family who'd attended De La Salle, Marcellin and Taylors College, came into contact with a 19-year-old hood from the wrong side of town. Hacker Harris was the classic psychopath – happy, smiling, a natural comic and joke-teller, yarn-spinner and liar with family connections and friendships from Thomastown to Collingwood.

Harris was strong as a bull, but was considered a dumb ox of a kid … a loudmouth liar whose wild comic yarns ran between fact and fiction until the listener could no longer tell the difference. There was only one point on which Harris never told a lie. That was his almost magical ability to make firearms appear out of nowhere with a wave of his drinking hand. In 1974, the young 16-year-old Alfonse Cologne had never seen a real handgun. He was about to try to sell a replica .45 calibre to a madman who was carrying a sawn-off shotgun.

The whole thing was so childish and the brawl that followed so predictable. The only sad thing in the whole affair was that Al Cologne had paid $300 for the .45-calibre replica, on the firm understanding that it was real. He tried to sell it on to Harris, still thinking it was real.

What followed the wild brawl that erupted was even stranger than Cologne's stupidity: Harris accepted Cologne's story of being conned and then gave Cologne his first true-blue firearm free of charge. It was a double-barrel sawn-off hammer-action 1938 shotgun. A classic cut-down masterpiece with a pistol grip and a box of solid load shells. In one fell swoop, young Al Cologne was no longer just a kid with a dream, but an armed kid with a dream. So the story begins ...

H Division of Pentridge Prison was then the toughest, bloodiest, hardest division in the most blood-soaked prison in Australia. Hacker Harris, Jimmy Lochrie, Danny Johnson and a handful of hand-picked psychopaths were in the middle of a prison gang war that began in 1975. Harris headed up a prison gang nicknamed 'The Raincoat Men' because when it rained they never got wet as Harris had secured the backing of the Governor of Security.

The H Division screws had to be seen to be believed. They were mindless, violent thugs who relished blood, a far cry from screws of the modern era. The modern-day lot would not be physically tough enough to pour a cup of tea for the jaw-breakers that worked in H Division Pentridge during the 1950s, 1960s and 1970s.

Jimmy Lochrie asked Hacker a question: 'Have you ever looked into a mirror and seen your clear reflection, then reached out to touch it only to realise that there was no mirror there at all?'

Hacker Harris stared at his friend and thought for a moment, before answering. 'No Jim, I haven't.'

'Well, I have,' replied Jim.

Jimmy Lochrie was quite insane and a conversation with him often fluttered off into the shadow of the valley of rubber-room magic.

Hacker looked at Jim and said, 'I've been thinking of cutting my left hand off, mate, and getting one of them stainless-steel pirate's hooks, like the old Captain Hook.'

Jim nodded, as if it was the most sensible thing he'd heard all day. Maybe it was. Then he topped Hacker's little brainwave with one of his own. 'Vincent Van Gogh had the right idea,' he said slowly. 'He couldn't paint for shit, but because he cut his ear off he wrote himself into the pages of history.'

Hacker nodded. 'Yeah, you're right there, mate,' he said. 'The world is full of one-handed men, but there ain't no buggers I ever heard of in the Melbourne criminal world with no ears.'

'Yeah,' said Jim, 'food for thought. Food for thought.'

'Anyway,' replied Hacker, 'enough of this shit ... who's got the tomahawk?'

'I have,' said Danny.

'Well, give it here. We'll give it a mocka in the shower yard after lunch.'

Jimmy smiled.

Danny looked worried.

Hacker Harris just looked blank. For him, the Raincoat War was a war he started, backed by a gang he'd created, against enemies he'd hand-picked. It was a war he knew he couldn't lose.

Harris was a young man with a dream, too. An insane dream – to not only become the most feared criminal in Melbourne, but also the most hated – and nothing and no one would prevent Hacker Harris from reaching out and touching this dream.

The old saying 'Beware of what you wish for because it might come true' had not yet filtered through to the mind of the young psychopath. So, too, does another story begin.

17 January 1998

Micky D'Andrea, Joe Gatto, Bobby MacNamara and Johnny Moore sat in silence as D'Andrea's wife took the phone call from Geoff 'Mumbles' Kindergarten. Micky D'Andrea never spoke on telephones and, as a result, his wife Vicki spent a lot of her time taking phone messages ...

'Bowling ball?' said Vicki. 'I don't understand.' Then she went silent and began to cry.

'Dead?' she whimpered. 'How? What? But who'd do that? And why?'

'What's going on? asked Micky.

'It's Alfonse,' cried Vicki. 'The cock suckers killed him.'

Micky hung his head like a man who had received sad news. He had already heard the news before, but didn't say anything. Joe Gatto did the same. Johnny Moore and Bobby MacNamara, however, screamed in anger, outrage and shock. They couldn't believe it. At once, Moore rang the silent home phone number of his friend and hero, Alfonse Cologne. A policeman answered and explained that Mrs Cologne had been given medication by the family doctor and couldn't come to the phone.

'By the way, Johnny,' said the cop, 'we want to talk to you.'

Johnny Moore hung up. The unbelievable had happened. The death of a legend is always more unbelievable than it is sad. The whole thing was totally mind-numbing. Someone must have switched off the security system. It had to be a friend who was the last to see him alive.

'God,' said Johnny, 'if Al's gone, we're all fucked.'

Joe Gatto looked into the eyes of Micky D'Andrea and spoke softly in Italian.

D'Andrea nodded.

'What's going on?' yelled Moore.

D'Andrea looked at Moore and replied, 'Some of us are fucked, Johnny, some of us aren't. Let's just wait and see.'

'Wait and see be fucked!' yelled Moore. 'We gotta hit back!'

'Hit who?' asked Gatto softly. 'Hit the wind, hit the rain? We can only hit an enemy we can see. Come on.'

'So who do we hit?' Moore continued, frustrated and frightened. He began to cry. 'Hacker Harris – we'll kill him.'

'But he's in jail,' said Gatto patiently, as if he was talking to a retarded child.

Young Johnny Moore had once bashed the wife of Mumbles' best mate, Brian Carl Hanlon, and Alfonse had protected Moore from Hanlon's revenge. Suddenly, a wave of past sins and old scores was flooding into the paranoid, speed-ravaged mind of young Johnny Moore.

Workman, what about his crew? And Harris, that old no-eared mental case. The Albanians ... shit, the whole world was caving in on young Johnny. He went to the bathroom and rolled up his shirtsleeves. A good blast of speed would clear his head. That's what he needed.

'Why? Why?' he muttered, as he slid the needle into his arm and pushed the plunger. Who? Why? None of it made any sense. Suddenly, Johnny felt very frightened and paranoid. 'Alphonso,' he cried, as he looked into the bathroom mirror, tears in his eyes. 'I love you, mate – goodbye.'

11 December 1997

A newspaper reporter named Ray Jackson was visiting Hacker Harris in prison. Old Hacker was due for release on 12 February 1998, and Ray thought he could get a scoop.

Hacker had become a legend simply by living up to his motto 'the man who wins the game is the man who lives the longest'. Having survived 23 years in various prisons in two different states and several gang wars, both in and out of prison, Hacker had achieved his boyhood dream. He had become the most feared and by far the most hated man in the Melbourne criminal world.

Hacker had never lost his scallywag sense of comic fun and still spun wild yarns that ran from fact to fiction. As he had always said, 'Bullshit baffles brains. Tell a thousand men a different story each and no one will ever know what you're really up to.'

Ray had also done some stories on another Melbourne underworld criminal legend, Alfonse Cologne, and thought it would be good to get the two enemies of more than 20 years together for a photo session and television interview. When this was put to him, the old no-eared madman just smiled and replied, 'Al will not live that long. Now remember this, because, when it happens, and it *will* happen, I want you to remember that I told you first: Alphonso will be dead before I get out of jail. Believe me. I will live longer than him. The grave that fuck is going into has already been dug.'

Ray Jackson could not believe this. After all, Hacker was a famous leg-puller, joke-teller and yarn-spinner. Then again, old Hacker had two natural gifts: getting hold of guns and predicting the death of others. Ray Jackson was left wondering if he had just been handed the criminal inside tip of the year or whether he was the victim of the psychopath's black sense of humour. With Hacker, one could never be quite sure, as many a true word was said in jest and Harris was a great player of psychological mind games. The two men parted company with one man smiling at a 'joke' he knew would come true and the other deeply puzzled.

Alfonse Cologne was standing in the laundry of his $500,000 fortress of a home in Templestowe. Geoff 'Mumbles' Kindergarten had just left – he said he had to pop out for a packet of smokes.

'Back in 10 minutes,' said Geoff. But 10 minutes turned into something approaching 40 or 45 minutes. For some reason, the security alarm system had been turned off.

Three men walked into the back of the house. Big Al looked up to see his old friend and partner, Big Mick Conforte, with another long-time friend, Mad Charlie Hajalic, in the company of a third man, a short thick-set man he had known for years. But a man he didn't want in his home for all that.

Alfonse was not yet in fear – he was just surprised at this unexpected and uninvited visit. 'Hey,' he said, frowning.

The short, thickset man replied, 'Jesus wants ya for a sunbeam, pretty boy,' and with that pulled out his snub-nose .38 and sent a volley of shots into the big man's body.

Alfonse staggered and fell with a look of surprise.

Just then a fourth man entered the laundry yelling, 'Fuck it all – not the bloody body, the fucking head!'

'Jesus Christ,' said the newcomer, a blue-eyed man. 'If you want a job done, do it yourself.' He grabbed the gun from the short, thick-set Albanian, and pumped three shots into Big Al's head.

The four men then turned and ran. They jumped into a 1987 Ford LTD driven by a fifth man.

'Hey, let me out round the corner,' yelled Conforte. 'No one said anything about killing anyone. We was supposed to talk. All we was supposed to do was talk.'

Charlie turned to Conforte. 'Shut up, you weak prick. You knew what the go was. It's too late to start crying now.'

The LTD pulled up and Conforte clambered out and disappeared. 'Let me off further up the road,' said Charlie. 'Big Mick is waiting for me.'

'Which Mick?' asked Rod Attard, the driver of the LTD. 'Not the brain-dead body builder. Jesus, don't tell him nothing.'

'Nah,' said Charlie. 'It will all fall back on Mumbles. I can't believe he went for all this. The old apple cucumber. Fuck, when will they learn?'

As Charlie left the car, the Albanian spoke to him in Yugoslav. 'If you love your mother, you'll take this secret to your grave.'

Charlie nodded. He didn't need to be told twice.

'Well,' said Rod, 'we have just killed a hundred birds with a single stone. We evened up a hundred scores and a nice getting out of jail pressie for Hacker.'

'Poppa Dardo's dying wish granted,' he continued, 'and Charlie and Conforte left to mop up the gravy. The Black Diamond and Gilbert Bazooka get their revenue and half the drug informers in Melbourne lose their biggest protector. The rest of the boys can pull it all back together.'

The blue-eyed man said nothing in reply. He had only one reason and this had nothing to do with power struggles, money, crime or blood feuds. He was just doing an old friend a favour. The blue-eyed man smiled. The apple cucumber, a psychological tactic the Texan invented and Hacker Harris perfected, was to use a friend of the target to get close enough to kill.

Poor Kindergarten. Oh, well, you can't bury an Italian omelette without shooting and breaking a few eggs. Ha ha.

17 November 1977

Hacker Harris was out of Pentridge and going for a birthday drink at the Dover Hotel just a stone's throw from the Russell Street Police Station. He entered the hotel with two lifelong friends, a Jew named Benny David and an Italian from Mallazzo, Sicily, named Sammy Stromboli. Little Sammy was carrying a large bag containing an original World War II British-made 9mm Sten machine gun, a carbine Mark 1. A classic and most rare model. He planned to sell the weapon to Alfonse Cologne for $1,000. Hacker Harris didn't want it, as he already had a dozen 9mm M44 sub-machine guns, all fitted with 36-round box magazines. He even had 71-round drum magazines.

Hacker Harris boasted the largest collection of arms and ammo in Melbourne. He wouldn't pay $1,000 for a worn-out Sten gun, famous for jamming after the third shot and therefore not safe in the hands of the untrained. There was a slight trick to using the Sten, namely that it was damn near impossible to get ammo for it in 1977. Hacker knew that the 50 rounds the Sten came with were all there ever would be. This was a secret he didn't share with his friend Stromboli or Alfonse Cologne, the mug about to pay a grand for it.

The three men walked up the stairs to the lounge dance area of the pub and greeted Big Al Cologne, Tony Mavric, Big Mick Conforte and Ronnie Burgess with smiles and handshakes. Al Cologne and Harris pretended friendship, but secretly distrusted each other. When Cologne and Conforte saw the little Sicilian, Stromboli, they became so polite it was embarrassing.

Both Cologne and Conforte claimed Sicilian family connections. However, they were, in fact, Calabrians by way of Milan. Neither of them could even speak Italian to a full-blood Sicilian. Stromboli was part of an old Melbourne Sicilian clan with connections to the Monza and Caprice families. Yet little Sammy never needed to mention the word Mafia. The Mafia word was only used by men who came from mainland Italy and used the fact they were Italian as a reason to bluff their enemies.

In Sammy's opinion, Big Al was '*a prezzo Fisso*', a *scarchi* (Sicilian slang) expression for a menu, meaning a man who is easy to read. In other words, you saw Big Al coming, and his manner, style, strategy and tactics never changed. As Sammy said, 'If Al is a Sicilian, I'm a fucking Chinaman and I doubt he is even a Calabrian. He speaks Italian with a Milano accent.

'*Quanto costa?*' said Alfonse in Italian, meaning 'How much is it?'

'A thousand,' grunted Sammy.

'I'll give you 500 bucks,' said Al.

'I'll give your mother my dick in her arse,' answered Sammy and with that promptly walked out, leaving Hacker Harris and Benny David standing in shock. Benny was quickly told by Hacker to rush after the hot-headed little Sicilian and bring him back. Hacker remained drinking with Cologne and his crew.

'Have you seen Shane Goodfellow?' asked Cologne.

'Fuck Goodfellow,' replied Harris. 'Next time I see him, I'm going to snap his neck. This conversation is giving me the shits. Where's the dunny?'

With that, Harris marched off to the toilet, which was a natural enough reaction to Alfonse Cologne.

The toilet door at the Dover Hotel was made of wood with a little slide bolt to lock it. Hacker locked the door and pulled his pants down and proceeded to punish the porcelain. Then it happened. The toilet door was kicked open and a hail of punches rained down on Hacker. Blood and pain didn't bother Harris much, so, while he was being punched and kicked in the face, his only concern was to wipe his arse and pull his pants up. One still had to follow the rules of hygiene, even in a fist-fight.

It was only then that Hacker returned fire with a volley of punches that sent Cologne running. Kicking the shit out of Hacker Harris as he sat on the toilet was one thing, fighting him toe to toe was quite another.

The three men ran from the pub. Hacker was covered in so much blood that he could no longer see who or what he was punching. He blindly attacked two bouncers who had tried to come to his rescue. The night ended with little Jock Mackenzie, an old Collingwood crim, coming to Hacker's rescue.

After pulling out an old Italian 9mm Glisneti, 1910 model, a self-loading pistol not unlike the 7.65mm German Luger in appearance, Jock gathered up the bleeding and confused Harris and bundled him into a taxi. They headed for the safety of good old Collingwood.

Upon hearing the yarn told by Harris of the attack in the toilet at the hands of Italians, Mackenzie took off into the night, leaving Harris in the safety of friends. Poor old Jock Mackenzie was never seen again.

So begins another story.

Mackenzie was a clan Scot with heavy-duty relatives, all of them armed to the teeth. The Mackenzie motto read: 'From the lonely shielding of the misty mountains, divide us. A waste of wild seas, yet still the blood is strong. The heart is highland and we in our dreams behold the Hebrides.'

Jock Mackenzie's death that dark night could not be pinned on Alfonse Cologne. However, the Mackenzies demanded the revenge of an old Aussie Collingwood criminal family, and they took it as a fact that Al had something to do with it. Which is why Harold Kindergarten, a nephew of old Jock's, attacked Alfonse in a Footscray nightclub two nights later. He almost beat the big Italian to a pulp and only eased off when the police arrived.

Harold was locked up and it was at this stage that Harold cried out, 'You fuckin dog, Alfonse.'

Harold was later to hang himself in the Footscray police cells. The 'dog' remark was soon forgotten, but not the death of the young Kindergarten.

The shovel that was to dig Alfonse's grave was selected on that night.

The secret of reaping the greatest
Fruitfulness and the greatest enjoyment
From life is to live dangerously! – Nietzsche

November 1966

A 12-year-old Hacker Harris sat in silence in the Greensborough Seventh Day Adventist Church on a Saturday morning. The preacher, Pastor Pat Ford, poured fire and brimstone into the congregation.

'And the Beast will arise and swallow us all to its bowels, lest we heed the warnings of Ellen G White and the Book of Revelation and run to the hills,' he thundered.

This was classic Jim Reeves, 'Gimme that old-time religion' stuff. The Pope and the Catholic Church were supposed to be planning to take over the World. Only guts, guns and God would defeat the Sons of Satan.

Young Hacker sat in terrified silence. The Seventh Day Adventists, sometimes called the Christian Jews, believed in a fundamental Old Testament hellfire and brimstone brand of religion that no one outside the Church could understand. Next to the King James Bible in the boot of young Hacker's father's car was a mint-condition German Bergmann 9mm MP 18 sub-machine gun complete with

500 rounds of ammo. Young Hacker was taught Bible and guns from childhood and, as a result of perverted religious teachings, saw Rome as the centre of all evil, the Pope and the Catholic Church as the 'head' of the Beast, as revealed in the last book of the Bible, the book of Revelation.

'Yes, you!' cried the preacher, pointing at young Hacker. 'Yes, you, young Michael Brendon. Don't look away, lad. I'm talking to you!' screamed the preacher.

Michael Brendon Harris, known to all his mates as Hacker, looked at the old preacher in horror and shock.

'Jesus wants you, son,' cried the preacher man. 'What does Jesus want you for?'

'I don't know,' murmured the terrified Hacker.

'A sunbeam, lad. That's what Jesus wants you for, boy. Jesus wants you for a sunbeam.'

15 January 1998

'The point blank M-94 vest is designed for tactical officers who require functional, yet versatile load-carrying capabilities. The pockets are compatible with today's state-of-the-art tactical equipment and are also positioned to ensure maximum convenience for both left- and right-handed officers. Adjustable retention loops are built in. In addition, an adjustable radio pocket on the back of the vest accommodates virtually any tactical communications equipment. As a completely customised alternative, the M-94 is available with a modular grid system of Velcro and snaps allowing the wearer to determine the placement of pouches and pockets according to the demands of his or her mission.

'For upgraded protection, class 3 or class 4, hard armour plates can be inserted into the back plate pockets. Design features are heavy-duty, military special nylon outer shell, and universal radio carrier, built in front and back hard armour place pockets, Velcro removable identification on front and back for convenient carrying of additional equipment. Extensive upper-body protection, including shoulders, adjustable side-closure system, three tactical-equipment-carrying pockets, canalisation for radio, wire systems or flexible plastic restraints are standard features. Options include nomex, fire-retardant, outer shell ballistic collar protection, ballistic groin protector, class 3 and class 4 hard armour plates, cordura carry case and a modular grid system is also available.

'The standard colours are: black, navy, olive, grey and camouflage.

'Ballistic material threat level: Kevlar one. Spectra three and Hi-Lite two.

'This concludes today's lecture, ladies and gentlemen.'

Detective Inspector 'Big Jim' Reeves rose to his feet and turned to Detective Chief Superintendent Charlie Ford. 'I'll stick to what I've got,' he said, tapping his shirt, which was tucked in over the top of his concealable body armour vest. 'A Spectra concealable ballistic vest.'

'Fuck it,' said Charlie. 'Most crooks couldn't hit the side of a barn with a shovel full of wheat. I'll go without. By the way, what's the latest on Alfonse?'

Big Jim smiled and nodded. 'Tomorrow night, so I'm told. Ha! Ha! Ha!'

'Well' said Charlie. 'Bloody well hope so. Ten fucking years overdue but better late than never. Who's pulling the trigger?'

'I don't know,' said Big Jim. 'All Mumbles told me was the Italian's off tomorrow night.'

'Good,' said Charlie. 'He's had his run. You know what they say … every dog has his day.'

With that, the two old dinosaur cops laughed like pre-historic hyenas and left for the pub where they planned to partake of a mixed grill with the lot, and a dozen or so pints as per their general lunchtime requirements.

6 February 1986

Brian Carl Hanlon stood at the telephone in Bendigo Prison. With tears in his eyes, he listened to his wife pour out her story of brutal violence and rape at the hands of a punk teenage kid from the western suburbs.

The offender was a young would-be gangster named Johnny Moore, the spoiled son of old Sixpence Moore, the SP bookie. Moore felt his dad's old dockie and criminal connections entitled him to run riot in the nightclubs of Melbourne. His new friendship with the great Alfonse Cologne and his Lygon Street plastic mafia crew had added weight to the young kid's ambitions.

Brian hung up the phone and returned to his cell to find a phone number.

'Come on. Where is it? Where is it?' he muttered over and over. He was shaking with anger at what his wife had told him, and could hardly think straight.

Tony MacNamara and Hacker Harris walked into the cell to see a tearful Hanlon fumbling through his personal belongings.

'What's up?' asked Tony.

'You got Mumbles's phone number?' Brian said, his voice cracking.

'Nah,' replied Tony, 'but I can get it for you.'

'Well, get it then,' said Hanlon. 'I need to talk to Mumbles urgently.'

'OK,' said Tony. He was surprised, but knew better than to intrude too much.

There was a long silence. Brian had tears rolling down his cheeks.

'Stop crying, Brian,' Tony said after a while. 'What's wrong? What's the matter?' he asked gently.

That's when Brian told him.

Seven days later, old Sixpence Moore was forced to pay a cash compensation to members of the Hanlon and Kindergarten families in return for the life of his spoiled-brat punk junkie kid.

Honour was preserved, as they say, but nothing was ever forgotten. Alfonse Cologne, acting as the go-between, took the cash from Old Man Moore and handed it to Mumbles. Mumbles in turn handed it over to the Hanlons. What Alfonse was not to know in 1986 was that acting as the go-between, and, in doing so, protecting young Moore, would form part of the shadow that would see him to his grave.

14 October 1986

Hacker Harris was yet again back on the streets of Melbourne. The now not-so-young street fighter, gunman and standover man had earned himself the bloodiest and most violent reputation in

Melbourne for gunplay, torture, death and insane comedy. He had the backing of old Tex Longman and Poppa Dardo, the King of the Albanian criminal world in Melbourne. Harris saw himself in the gunslinger light. More a Gary Cooper than an Al Capone. Harris was usually broke but always armed to the teeth. Another gang war for the sheer comedy of it was about to start. Naturally, Hacker turned his undivided attention to the major heroin dealers of Melbourne, most of whom called Al Cologne their friend. This suited Cologne, as he could cut himself in for a slice of a hundred different pies. It also suited Harris because it's easy to shoot fish if they all swim in the same pond. So the games began.

For Alfonse this was not his 'cup of tea'. He hadn't fought his way up the ladder to squabble with a mental case over a $2,000-a-week sling, which was all Hacker wanted. So, while paying the cash in secret, he loudly verbalised his wish to kill Harris. Meanwhile, Harris generally left Cologne alone and ran riot among the lesser lights within the Melbourne drug world. Those who didn't pay up some form of cash tribute were cut up, shot up, burned out or killed. Alfonse was being pressured to make some sort of stand against the madman who lived in Collingwood. Alfonse had become a glamour gangster and what on earth was he meant to do against Harris. Attack him with his American Express Card? Face, however, had to be saved, so some form of showdown had to come. It had been coming for a long, long time.

Cologne had been able to sway a lot of Harris's old friends over to his side – or so it appeared at the time. The Kindergartens, Monzas, Strombolis and the Caprice Clan, Mad Charlie Hajalic and Rod Attard. It seemed to Harris that the power of drug money had perverted everyone. Alfonse had Boris the Black Diamond, Gilbert Bazooka and half the old dockie families in tow. Even the Mackenzies didn't want to back Harris against the Lygon Street Mafia. Only the Albanians and Benny David agreed to back Hacker, along with a small crew of armed Robbery Squad coppers who had a running battle with the Major Crime Squad at the time. The whole thing was getting quite complicated. But, as Harris said, 'When in doubt – shoot everyone.'

'Ultimately, people like Alfonse are killed by their friends, not their enemies. His mistake was that he could no longer tell the difference.' – Hacker Harris.

CHAPTER 2

FAMILY BUSINESS

Alfonse stank of his favourite,
poofy after-shave.

February 4, 1987

SAMMY Stromboli sat in a flat in West Melbourne. He had become addicted to heroin and was waiting for his new friend and adviser, Alfonse Cologne, to visit him. Big Al used Sammy as a 'taster'. Every time Al collected a fresh shipment of smack from Gilbert or Micky Wong or Boris, Sammy would try it out. He had originally hated Alfonse but the heroin had turned Alfonse from an enemy into a friend. Sammy had rejected his whole family for the love of heroin and, by extension, of Alfonse.

A tall, blonde girl danced slowly in front of Sammy. She looked like a long-legged, high-fashion catwalk model, but one that was smacked out. She had what they call heroin chic. She was wanton and lewd – '*lascivo*', as the Italians say. Yet her hips and tits were wide and lavish and she had the eyes and mouth '*Di La Lapilli*', or ashes from a volcano. Her name was Mandy and she looked all of 18 or 19 years old. She was, however, a tender 14 years old and had been addicted to heroin for 12 months. This was thanks to her 'Uncle' Alfonse, who was, in fact, no blood relation at all. Her mother had married Mushie Peas and a few people knew that in reality she was the baby daughter of Ray Kindergarten. Had Alfonse known this, he might not have been so keen to slide a heroin needle into her arm.

For an Italian to understand the complexity of inter-relations between the old Australian criminal families would be as difficult as an Aussie trying to guess who was related to whom in Italy – even if the Aussie was born in Italy. Alfonse was and would always remain outside of the 'inside'. He was '*Lucido*' as the *scarchi* Sicilians put it – meaning 'shoe polish', a slang expression meaning 'all looks and no guts'. Alfonse was in many ways simply a '*Giornaliero*' – in Sicilian slang this meant a journeyman. He was not really a crime boss or Mafia don. He was simply a lover of '*Cattiveria*' or wickedness. He was a power junkie and, with drugs and violence, backed by the shadow of the Mafia myth, he exerted power over the weak within the criminal world. Having Sammy Stromboli hooked on smack, Alfonse could control the thinking of the whole Stromboli clan, as Sammy was the favourite son of Frank Stromboli and grandson of old Poppa Nicolo Stromboli. To control Sammy was to have influence over the Stromboli family and their restaurants and nightclub interests in Lygon and King Streets.

As for Mandy, Sammy's junkie girlfriend, she would be useful in one of the parlours in Carlton. Alfonse owned most of them. At least, that's the way Al saw it.

Ah, Australia, thought Alfonse. What a wonderful country!

Alfonse entered the flat and was greeted with smiles all round as he pulled out an ounce of pure china-white heroin from the pocket of his $2,000 Italian sports coat. He was in a hurry. His BMW sports car was parked outside with the engine running and Carlo Muratore at the wheel. Muratore was part of the old Victoria Market Mafia clans of the late Domenico 'The Pope' Italiano, Vincenzo Muratore and Vincenzo Agillette – three Calabrian clans who sometimes had to be pulled into line by the Sicilians, who allowed the Calabrian, Milano and Roman show-offs to play gangsters and swagger about like movie stars. Providing they took the risks and made the money, they would receive the Sicilian blessing.

Alfonse stank of his favourite poofy aftershave and expensive cologne. It was said that at night you could smell Alfonse coming down a dark alley in Carlton from a distance of 60 yards, especially if a good breeze was blowing towards you.

Alfonse tossed the ounce bag on the coffee table and said, 'Let me know what you think, Sammy,' before turning to leave. Mandy ran to the kitchen to grab a fix and a spoon. Alfonse averted his head as he opened the door and muttered, 'Junkie dogs, I hate them.' Shrugging his shoulders, he closed the door behind him. 'Well,' he mused, 'you need manure to grow a rose.'

Alfonse was off to Santino's restaurant for a glass or two of Shiraz and a nice plate of chicken lasagna with salad. He had a meeting with Mad Charlie, Hacker Harris's old mate-turned-traitor. He, like Charlie, didn't completely trust anyone who had anything to do with Harris, regardless of how long ago contact might have been. Shane Goodfellow, Gilbert and Gonzo wanted to see him.

Goodfellow had turned from one of Melbourne's top blood and guts street fighters into a junkie, and Gilbert owed his loyalty to Boris the Black Diamond. However, Harris had almost killed Goodfellow in H Division, Pentridge in 1979.

The enemy of my enemies is my friend, Big Al thought to himself. The politics of it all. I love it.

Later that night, at the Pasta Rustica, with Goodfellow, Gilbert and Gonzo knocking back large plates of baby lamb and bottles of Rosso Vino red wine, the waiter whispered in Big Al's ear.

'Jesus Christ on a fucking bike,' said Alfonse.

Noticing that Al had turned pale, Gilbert asked, 'What's up?'

'Sammy Stromboli and Mandy have been taken to the Western General Hospital and pronounced dead on arrival,' he answered. He looked stunned.

'How come?' asked Gonzo.

'Smack overdose,' replied Alfonse.

Goodfellow went silent. He knew who Mandy Peas really was and knew the significance of a whisper in Big Al's ear. If this overdose had anything to do with Al, thought Shane, the Kindergartens had better not put any of this shit together or there would be a lot of dead people.

Al paid the bill from a wad of hundred-dollar notes thick enough to choke an elephant, and walked out. It was clear he was not a happy man. He didn't care less about Mandy. But what the hell was he going to tell Poppa Stromboli?

> 'The man who plants the seed gets to chop the tree.'
> – MAD CHARLIE

Hacker Harris and old Poppa Dardo, the Albanian crime boss, sat in the lounge room of Poppa Nicolo Stromboli's home in West Footscray. Sammy's father, Frank, was also in attendance. Alfonse had been trying to cut himself a little Albanian influence by supplying one of old man Dardo's son's with heroin. Old Poppa Dardo and Poppa Stromboli had known each other since they had arrived in Australia on the same ship in 1957. Italy had become a second home or first port of call for Albanians escaping the Communist regime in Albania.

Harris had just shot one of Alfonse Cologne's top drug movers in the western suburbs (and right-hand man of Gilbert Bazooka) in the stomach for daring to raise his voice in anger to one of Poppa Dardo's sons. Hacker's friendship with the Strombolis went back to Thomastown in the early 1960s, where the family lived in with relatives before upgrading the accommodation to West Footscray.

'This a fucking cocksucker,' snarled Poppa Stromboli. 'Di Inzabella say Alfonse OK. He's a good boy. Please I beg you, no touch. No touch.'

Bottles of 'grappa' and large slices of aglio gorgonzola (garlic cheese) and affuicatao salmone (smoked salmon) were in plentiful supply with sliced cetriolo and cipolle (cucumber and onions). Large plates of hot salami, gnocchi with a strong tomato butter and garlic sauce remained virtually untouched. The only man eating was Hacker Harris, whose consumption of the fare with such gusto prompted Old Poppa Stromboli to stop crying and laugh loudly.

'Buon appetito. Enjoy, enjoy!' he said.

At this Hacker stopped eating and patted his stomach. 'Non *posso mangiare, Poppa. Sono a dieta* [I cannot eat, Poppa. I'm on a diet],' he said to the old man.

The sadness in the room was broken with laughter.

'Maybe a little connoli?' asked Poppa Stromboli.

'No,' replied Hacker. 'I don't want to be a porko grando.'

Everyone laughed. Then the tone turned serious again.

'Sammy, stupido boy. Fucking junkie. But Alfonse he swear to me he take good care of Sammy. Now he is in da grave. Mamma mia. Holy Madonna. Someone gonna pay for this. De Inzabella, he say it's not the fault of Alfonse. Fucking Calabrian Milano dogs. Someone is going to pay for this,' cursed Poppa Dardo.

He looked at Hacker and gave a sly wink. Another part of the jigsaw that would paint the picture of Cologne's death had been found.

'What was the first movie Marilyn Monroe ever did?' asked Hacker Harris.

Bobby Kindergarten and Charlie Mackenzie sat in silence. Then Benny David piped up, '*Scudda Hoo, Scudda Hay* in 1948.'

Harris was impressed and handed over $100.

Sitting at the bar of the Builders Arms Hotel in Fitzroy in the midst of a raging gang war, doing a Marilyn Monroe movie trivia quiz was hardly what one would expect. But men who shoot other men for a living tend to chat about the most offbeat nonsense.

'OK,' said Benny. 'What was the seventh movie Marilyn ever made?'

'*All About Eve*, 1950,' replied Hacker with a smirk.

Benny David handed the $100 back.

'I've got one none of you can answer,' said Alfonse as he walked in. 'What was the last movie Marilyn ever made?' With that, he landed a smashing right-hand punch to Benny David's jaw, knocking him out cold.

The three men Alfonse was with proceeded to engage Mackenzie in fisticuffs. Punches flew in all directions while Harris and Cologne were locked in rock and roll in a long overdue street fight. Alfonse swung fast and wild, aiming at Harris's head. This was a mistake, as Harris had a head like a mallet, able to withstand pain like few others. Harris was a strong, slow puncher who liked to move in close and then grab hold. Once he grabbed hold, there was no letting go. With his face covered in blood, Harris picked Alfonse up and physically tossed him through the hotel door, following through with kicks when Al fell into the gutter.

Local police were called, along with an ambulance, but none of the combatants needed either, and insisted it had been a friendly bit of fun with each man covered in his own blood.

As Alfonse and his companions walked away, Harris yelled, '*Something's Got To Give*, 1962, and it was the last movie she ever made and she never finished it. You will never live to finish yours either, maggot. I'll outlive the fuckin' lot of you!'

Alfonse had guts and, in his own way, was as brave as a lion.

However, any man strong enough to stand a 30-punch onslaught to the face, then pick Alfonse up and hurl him through a pub door into the gutter wasn't going down easily. Alfonse had based his entire reputation on nightclub brawling and had never been physically lifted off the ground and hurled like a rag doll out a door in his life. More's the pity. If he had, he may not have believed he was unbeatable. Overconfidence led to his death as much as the plots of his friends and enemies. Gunplay was the only way to go with Harris – but not face to face. Harris might be slow with his fists but his reputation with a handgun was almost Wild West stuff. Harris would have to be got from behind and at night. As Alfonse walked away, he decided to kill Hacker Harris. But how?

He made his play two nights later. As Hacker walked alone down the darkness of Forest Street, Collingwood, a 1977 Ford LTD drove by. Three shots rang out from a .38-calibre revolver, missing him by inches. When slugs speed past the human head, you can actually hear a whistling noise. Harris didn't see Alfonse, but he blamed him for it. The game was set for a battle royal.

The following day, Hacker went to see Mad Charlie Hajalic in Caulfield. He told him of his plans for war.

'Leave me out of it, Hacker,' said his old friend. 'I'm involved with Alfonse and there is a lot of money at stake. A war would fuck us all up.'

'It wouldn't fuck me up,' said Hacker, poker-faced.

'Well, it would fuck me up, all right,' Charlie said shortly. 'I'm a businessman involved in crime, not some insane mental case. If you want war, you're one out, alone. No one will back you. You'll lose, mate. I'm telling you. Alfonse and his crew are too strong. You can't win.'

Hacker walked out of Charlie's house a bit despondent but all the more hell bent on the idea that, win, lose or draw, there was going to be a war ...

Hacker quietly sang to himself as he put the blowtorch to Eddie Decarlo's feet. Eddie screamed as the flame hit his toes. Torturing smack dealers for their money was smelly but a good earner. And when the smack and cash came out of Alfonse's pocket, it did indeed tickle Hacker's sense of comedy. While Hacker tortured Eddie in the cellar of a Port Melbourne hotel, Benny David and Vincent Gorr were ransacking his home in Footscray. They had located $60,000 in cash and drug gold.

Of course, the story of the so-called 'toe-cutting' job and robbery on Decarlo and then the total disappearance of Decarlo didn't take long to reach Alfonse's ears.

Big Al went into hiding whenever he heard Harris was in town. Harris would vanish, then reappear. He was virtually impossible to kill because he couldn't be pinned down to any habit or routine. His address was a mystery. Harris had become a physical and psychological shadow. He could find anyone but no one seemed to be able to find him. Gang war was all that Harris knew about and the criminal businessmen he was fighting had lost or forgotten the art of warfare. Drug money, wealth and criminal political power was their cup of tea. Blood and guts street combat after dark and the tactics and strategy involved was a stranger to them.

Ray Kindergarten sat holding a photo of his baby daughter, Mandy. The same girl that was Mushie Peas' drug-addict stepdaughter. Mushie had disowned her despite the fact that he himself did big amphetamine business with Gilbert, Gonzo and Alfonse.

Hacker Harris sat next to Ray.

'It's not right, Hacker. She was only a fuckin' kid,' he swore. Tears were running down Ray's face.

Hacker looked at the schoolgirl in the photo. He had met her once when she was being pushed in a pram. She was sucking on her dummy at the time. Little did Hacker think all those years before that little baby Mandy would grow up into a teenage junkie whore who spent her nights sucking on bigger dummies to pay for her heroin habit.

Drugs, thought Harris, not for the first time. They are fucking the whole country up.

'They reckon Big Al was plonking her,' cried Ray.

'I don't know about that,' said Harris out of fairness. 'But I do know Stromboli was and that Sammy was getting his gear from Alfonse.'

'That's good enough for me,' said Ray.

'What goes around comes around,' said Kindergarten, crying.

Hacker nodded and put his arm around Ray's shoulder in a gesture of comfort, smiling to himself. He had found one more nail to drive into the Calabrian coffin.

'Do you remember O Henry's stories?' asked Hacker gently.

Gilbert Bazooka shook his head. 'No, never heard of him.'

Harris told the O Henry yarn about a young married couple in the year of 1905. They were very poor but deeply in love with each other. The wife had long hair all the way down to her waist and the husband had a pocket watch his great-grandfather had given his grandfather and from him it had passed to the grandson. It was Christmas and both the wife and husband, so much in love, wanted to surprise each other with a gift of value. So the wife sold her lovely hair to a wig maker. With the money, she bought her husband a platinum chain for his pocket watch. Meanwhile, her husband sold his pocket watch to buy his wife a silver Spanish comb for her beautiful hair.

Gilbert looked puzzled. 'What are you trying to say, Hacker?' he asked.

'I'm not saying anything, mate,' said Hacker. 'It's just that, while you're busy doing something for someone else behind that person's back, you forget that maybe they are doing something as well. Good or bad, for better or worse, both can come out the loser.'

'What are you trying to say?' asked Gilbert again.

'Easy,' replied Hacker. 'If you don't surprise me, I won't surprise you.'

Gilbert still looked puzzled as Hacker walked away.

'Forget Alfonse, mate. He's not Father Christmas. Walk away and forget about doing anything behind anyone's back. Least of all, mine. OK, mate!'

Gilbert nodded but, as Harris walked away, he thought, Bloody O Henry. Harris talks in riddles but he gets his point across.

> 'In the midst of life, we are in death.'
> – ANON.

Lorraine Kindergarten sat in the bar of the Tower Hotel in Collingwood with Hacker Harris. They were talking football. Lorraine was doing most of it.

'1902. That was the first Premiership Collingwood ever won,' she said. 'Followed by 1903, 1910, 1911, 1919, 1927, 1928, 1929, 1930, 1935, 1936, 1953, 1958 and 1959.'

'Bullshit,' said Hacker. 'They never won 1959.'

'Well, who did then?' asked Lorraine.

'I don't know and I don't care. But it wasn't Collingwood. OK?' replied Hacker.

'Collingwood Brownlow Medallists,' continued Lorraine without drawing breath, 'were Coventry, 1927, then Collier in 1929, another Collier in 1930, Whelan in 1939, Fothergill a year later, Thompson in 1972 and Moore in 1979.'

Harris sat in silence, chewing things over for a moment. 'For a chick from Footscray, you sure know a lot about Collingwood, Lorrie,' he said at last.

Hacker always called Lorraine Kindergarten 'Lorrie'. Lorraine was a tough knockabout semi-criminal chick from a fully criminal family. Tall, long legs, big boobs and with golden long hair, she worked as a dancer and a stripper. That is when she wasn't driving the getaway car for bank robberies and jeweller's shop smash-and-grabs.

Lorraine laughed. '*O che sciabura d'essere sneza cogillioni*.'

'What?' asked Hacker.

'Oh what a misfortune to be without testicles,' Lorraine giggled. 'Voltaire said that.'

Lorraine was a strange chick. She travelled the world and had seen and done it all. She had once worked at the Kit Kat Ranch on Kit Kat Road, east of Carson City in Lyon County near Reno in Nevada. She had gone to America for a holiday in 1979 and married an Italian-American, Carmine Caprice. Her luck started to go downhill from that point on. Within three months, she was working at the Kit Kat Ranch.

This establishment was the oldest cathouse in Lyon County. The brothel is, or was, open 24 hours a day and the girls worked in 14-hour shifts. They did this for three consecutive weeks before having a week's break. The club had between 40 and 50 ladies working around the clock on different shifts. If you were to drive east on Highway 50 from Carson City about 6.5 miles (or approximately one mile past the Green Lyon County sign), you would see, on the right-hand side of the road, Sam's Saloon. Next to it, you would see a billboard announcing the three brothels on Kit Kat Road. By turning right on Kit Kat Road and continuing for a mile, you would reach Kit Kat Ranch. It was the first house on the left, with a cupid-pink exterior that made it hard to miss.

Lorraine didn't need to divorce her husband when she got sick of him. He was shot dead in New York City by an off-duty policeman. The reason for the shooting remained a mystery. However, the policeman in question had not long before then taken a holiday to Nevada, and the lovely Lorraine still smiles slyly whenever she mentions her husband and his untimely demise. She returned from America three years later with enough cash to buy three massage parlours outright and lease another four. She had done the hard work at the Kit Kat Ranch and was now a lady of personal wealth, not to mention a bit of local power as a result of her wealth. She paid Hacker a grand a week, not for protection, but for the friendship. If she ever found herself in trouble, however, she knew she could call on Hacker Harris and his crew.

But I digress.

'I lent $25,000 to Alfonse,' said Lorraine, 'and I've got the feeling I'm gonna get lashed.'

Hacker shook his head. 'He borrows money from everyone. What was it for?'

'Smack,' replied Lorraine.

'Serves you right,' said Hacker. 'I bet Alfonse told you the gear was seized on a drug raid and the money's gone.'

'Yeah,' answered Lorraine, suddenly looking interested as Hacker did his crystal-ball gazing. She'd seen plenty of balls, but precious few crystal ones.

Hacker shook his head again. 'You're smart enough to turn your pussy into a million dollars and dumb enough to fall for that bullshit. You'll never get your dough back,' said Hacker. 'That turd owes half of Melbourne money. He invests it, makes his profit, then lashes and lies his way out of the debt. He's been doing it all his life.'

Lorrie put her hand right on Hacker's lap and gave him a gentle squeeze. 'Do you reckon you can help me, Hacker? I'll write the 25 grand off as a bad loss, but Al reckons he will bottle my face if I don't come up with two grand a week protection.'

Hacker smiled. 'Just tell him you can't afford two grand 'cause you're already paying me three a week. Tell him that if he has a problem to come and see me.'

'OK,' replied Lorraine and gave him an extra big squeeze as she flashed a wide sexy smile. 'You look like a man who desperately needs to have the top knocked off it. Come on, mate. Let's get out of here.'

Hacker Harris and Lorraine Kindergarten got up and walked out.

Three days later Lorraine Kindergarten was found dead from a heroin overdose. Lorraine had never used heroin in her life. It was concluded someone must have felt that, if they couldn't have a slice, they would simply get rid of the pie. Nothing could be proven. Alfonse couldn't be linked to Lorraine's death. He even went to her funeral. Hacker never went to funerals, as he considered it bad luck. However, in one week, Alfonse had moved in on Lorraine's empire, cutting Harris completely out. Another battle won, but the war still raged.

Milan – or Milano, as the Italians call it – is the capital of the region of Lombardy. It is the second largest city in Italy and regarded as one of Europe's finest and most dynamic places. It measures 182 square kilometres and is a city of action, work and money, some of it legitimate.

Sitting in the sunshine on the Piazza Della Scala, three Milano men, Johnny, Michael and Frank Gangitano, sat, quietly drinking aniseed cordial, otherwise known as Sambuca. On the table were side plates of mussels, octopus and oysters. There was also a large plate of pepperoni salad. The three brothers were in the transport business and ran trucks from Milan to Calabria.

'What news of our *paisans*?' asked Johnny.

Michael laughed like a hyena. 'Young Alfonse, he wants to be the big boss. He has all them skippy hillbillies thinking he is Mafiosi.'

The three men roared with laughter. They thought Al was more Jerry Lewis than Dean Martin.

'That shifty Calabrese. He will either outsmart us all or maybe outsmart himself,' Frankie said.

'He sent us the money for three new trucks. He wants a slice of our pie in return for our blessing to run powder from Rome to the south.'

'Three trucks?' said Johnny. 'Tell the pig to make it six trucks and the blessing is his. But what about the men in Naples and Palermo?'

Michael sighed. 'Alfonse tells us not to worry. He reckons they don't matter.'

'You know what,' said Frank, 'I think we will get six trucks and Big Al will get a funeral. He's a smart boy but a stupid man.'

Johnny nodded. 'Ah well,' he said dryly. 'If Alfonse wants to be in the movies, let him. Maybe one day he will learn that life isn't a motion picture. Ha! Ha!'

Meanwhile, back in Australia, Hacker Harris was walking out of Bojangles nightclub on lower St Kilda Esplanade.

Shane Goodfellow, Graeme Jenson, Frankie Valastro and Ronnie Burgess sat in a car outside. You didn't have to be a brain surgeon to know that Alfonse had given the order for Harris to be killed. If you couldn't work that out, you would have needed a brain surgeon, or worse, an undertaker.

'Chequebooks don't win gang wars. You need dash, not cash.' – Chopper Read.

Killing a madman wasn't as simple as it sounded. A Turkish hanger-on attached to Goodfellow's crew conned Harris outside and Tony Mavric was hiding in the bushes with a shotgun. A shot rang out. The Turk hit the footpath, dead as a doornail with a .410 shotgun blast through the right eyeball. Goodfellow's wife jumped into the car while Tony Mavric sat in the bushes shitting his pants.

'He's fucking mad. He shot the Turk point blank, then pulled his dick out and pissed into the bushes all over Tony. The bloke's a fucking maniac,' exploded Goodfellow.

As the car sped away, Goodfellow knew he was in trouble. Alfonse was the only one who could protect him now.

Two weeks later, Harris was arrested for murder and, on Alfonse's advice and instructions, Goodfellow made a full statement to the Homicide Squad. Also on instructions, he agreed to go Crown

Witness against Harris. At last, Alfonse had rid himself of his worst and most hated enemy. Or so he thought.

'It is when power is wedded to chronic fear that it becomes formidable.' – Eric Hoffer (1954)

The years between 1987 and 1991 were for Alfonse Cologne the best years. He rose in wealth and power. Harris was in Pentridge Prison where, many would say, a mental case like him belonged. Alfonse was controlling one third of all heroin and methamphetamine sales in Melbourne nightclubs.

The new legal sex industry with its brothels, lap-dancing clubs, strip joints and Australian-financed porn films was growing. But the one criminal industry he couldn't gouge a foothold into was the illegal arms market. Hacker Harris and his crew had that sewn up. There wasn't big money involved but Harris and his hillbilly Aussie connections seemed to control this market. It seemed odd to Alfonse that even the guns he and his crew owned all came from people who bought guns from Hacker's people. But, he mused, this was Australia. To shoot your enemies you had to first buy your guns from them, as well as your ammo.

Melbourne is like that. A mix of Chicago-style gangsters, New York-style Mafia and an old tradition of feudal loyalty to local crime lords with traditional criminal clans and families dating back to the days of John Wren and Squizzy Taylor. It has a criminal sub-culture unlike any city in Australia, all within the sub-culture of the wider Australian criminal world. It is almost like East End London, with its inter-criminal family network and South London violence. Many so-called and would-be Godfathers and crime lords from other nationalities have come and gone – like rising comets that become falling stars. But the old ways, traditions and criminal culture remains. When the blood starts flowing, the Aussie, English, Irish and Scottish clans will all side with one another against any common foe. Melbourne is unique in Australia in that its criminal culture places the payback, vendetta and revenge along with its associated feuds and wars higher than anything, even money.

The Melbourne criminal culture never forgives nor forgets. The attitude of cutting the hand off to punish the offender's arm, regardless of cost, is ingrained in the old criminal families. A score may be repaid tomorrow, in 10 years' time or longer. One thing is certain – no old score is ever forgotten. The criminal payback vendetta holds an almost holy place in the minds of the men who live and die there. As one old Irishman said to me: 'The Italians invented the vendetta but the Irish make a bigger, bloodier mess.' Amen to that.

Hacker Harris, being the gun-happy, mental case he was, found himself yet again in prison in 1992 after getting out in 1991. Yet again it was related to a shooting charge. Harris got out of Pentridge Prison in November 1991 to find that Big Al had fled Melbourne along with his de facto wife and two children to Milan, Italy. The two events were not unrelated.

He returned to Melbourne in 1993, only after Harris had been convicted on the shooting charge after losing both State and High Court appeals. Naturally, Al laughed at the rumours he had taken himself and his family to Italy to avoid a blood war with Harris. He claimed he returned only because his father was dying from cancer. He said that the landmines placed in his driveway and discovered in 1991 (suspected to have been placed there on the orders of Harris) had little to do with his move to Italy the same year.

'That's a lie, a complete fallacy,' claimed Cologne to the media. 'The greater the lie, the more people believe it,' he said, quoting Adolf Hitler. It was a quote Cologne had picked up from Harris himself during the early 1970s. He also picked something else up, resulting in him having to shave his pubic hairs, but that is another story.

Al returned to a Harris-free state and a new and legal sex industry. Sex shops, brothels, escort services, adult bookshops, strip clubs, lap-dancing clubs and venues provided sexually explicit entertainment – all fully licensed by a grateful, greedy government keen to get its slice of the tax action. And they called Harris a standover man.

As a property developer, Big Al invested widely in all three areas using his shady business and legal contacts as front men, thus protecting himself behind a raft of paper companies. He had found a semi-legal way to push drug money through a legal washing machine, albeit a sleazy one.

He returned to his Saint Alfonse image by donating gifts of toys to the Royal Children's Hospital. A thousand bucks' worth of toys means a million bucks' worth of good will, a fact American Mafia worked out decades earlier. In America, the Hells Angels ran a public anti-drugs campaign while making speed to stick in kids' arms. Work that out. Big Al had cultivated an army of lawyers, business and legal contacts, high-flyers, even magistrates and judges. Police in some quarters spoke well of him, despite the fact that he had a nasty habit of bashing innocent young constables he caught off duty in a situation where he had the drop on them. Underneath, his old street habits stayed the same, and his violent streak meant that police were sometimes called, and this resulted in the management of various clubs banning Al from attendance.

He hadn't lost the plot – rather, the plot was starting to lose him. Older Italians and even Big Al's closest colleagues just shook their heads at a man who, on the one hand, was so brilliant and, on the other, so spoiled and childish.

Meanwhile, Al would sit in lap-dancing clubs with a semi-clad beauty between his legs and a handgun down his belt – or perhaps it was the other way around. Management and club security would stand dumbfounded as Big Al pulled his weapon out – and I don't mean his .38 – and instruct the dancer in question to loosen her G-string and sit on it, riding him up and down while members of the Cologne crew looked on and laughed. It was taken for granted that, when Alfonse and his Lygon Street team walked into any table-dancing club, they paid for nothing and, if Big Al or any member of his team dropped their zips, the dancer in question would have no choice but to either go down or sit on the offending member.

Al would infiltrate clubs he had no control over, using his friend and sometimes bodyguard, The Dasher. Dasher ran a security firm that supplied bouncers to most of the clubs in Melbourne. Al would see to it that professional call girls and high-class hookers were placed in certain clubs. A quick suck in the right place could take the sting out of certain investigations.

He could also screw up other clubs by using 'gypsy' dancers. These were chicks that went in for a week's work to one club – but did nothing but create trouble, teasing, starting fights, spreading drugs about, offering sex and generally creating a bloody uproar – including robbing clients – before vanishing to another club where the same game would be played. Having its reputation damaged by this would impact on the club. A licence was hard to get and easy to lose, and Al would capitalise on this.

It wasn't difficult to place underage drinkers and dancers in clubs not controlled by him, then organise for the police and assorted other inspectors to attend on the correct nights. Despite the fact that Big Al had been barred from most establishments, he still roamed freely with his small army of hangers-on. The result was brawls, shootouts, stabbings, attacks with pool cues and the blatant sexual abuse of lap dancers too frightened to complain. Alfonse was having a party in a playground.

What angered Alfonse was the influx of top-line, Penthouse-Pet types – former ballroom and professional dancers who were a threat to his control. They were well-educated, middle-class girls from good homes who were in the new table-top-dancing industry strictly for the cash. They would take no nonsense and would also lay a formal and legal complaint at the drop of a fly zipper.

Threats of sexual harassment cases and lawsuits from a younger generation of professional dancers who didn't seem to show any respect for Big Al or his crew were incomprehensible to Cologne. A financial investor in a club didn't welcome such changes. For example, a doctor's daughter from Perth who held a degree in economics, and who had taken up lap dancing for the tax-free cash, could earn $4,000 to $5,000 a week. This type of girl would not tolerate for a moment some would-be Robert De Niro Mafia impersonator pulling his ugly member out and yelling, 'Suck this, slut!'

It was starting to hit Big Al that he was no longer living in the 1970s or even the 1980s. Women's Liberation was no longer just a word but a way of life. Strippers who didn't use heroin or speed, strippers with bank accounts and lawyers, were giving his cosy criminal world a culture shock. Maybe violence would remind one and all just who he was. But, of course, it is difficult to win respect for violence when you continue to live under the shadow of a mental case like Hacker Harris.

So Big Al began to knock the smaller fish into shape and, for a time, he felt the 1970s and 1980s had returned. But, while Harris lived, Cologne would always remain a joke that was enjoyed behind his back.

'When will this stone be removed from my shoe?' Cologne complained to Poppa Brazzi. Like every other would-be gangster, he'd been watching too many *Godfather* films.

Poppa Brazzi was an old Sicilian who smiled at Alfonse but secretly didn't like him. '*Non capiso,*' he replied.

'Harris,' said Cologne sulkily, 'he is a stone in my shoe. When can I have the stone removed?'

Old Poppa Brazzi just smiled.

'*Un bicchierre di grappa,*' Alfonse muttered in Italian. The old man nodded and, with a wave of his hand, Big Al had a waiter appear with a cold bottle of Sicilian grappa.

'*Grato,*' said Poppa Brazzi.

'You want something to eat?' asked Big Al.

The old man thought, '*In insalata,*' he replied.

Again, Alfonse waved his hand before speaking. 'And the stone in my shoe?' he said again impatiently.

The old man smiled and said, 'For a bottle of grappa and a seafood salad, you come to me about Hacker Harris. "*Aiuto,* Poppa Brazzi."' The old man mimicked Alfonse, meaning 'Help'. He continued, '*Calabrese crostata di frutta,*' meaning 'Calabrian fruit pie', an insult directed at Alfonse. 'And you're a fucking Milano Calabrese. Hey, Porko, I tell you what, Alfonse. You want a stone out of your shoe? Remove it yourself, or take your shoe off. Otherwise, I think Harris will cut your feet off. Then you won't have shoes to put stones into. I can't help you,' the old man concluded.

'*Mi spiace,*' he said, meaning that he was sorry, but he didn't sound it.

Alfonse got up and walked away. Brazzi wouldn't dismiss Big Al so quickly unless, of course, Di Inzabella himself had turned his back on Alfonse. The Monzas and the Caprice family were all linked with the Stromboli clan. The Agillette family, the Italiano clan and the Muratores had all been doing business of late with the Dardo family, who were Albanian. Old Poppa Dardo was a friend of Hacker Harris. The ghost of Sammy Stromboli was coming back to tap Alfonse on the shoulder.

'Fuck 'em all,' said Big Al to himself. 'I've got the men, the money and the contacts. I'm tomorrow. They are all yesterday.' He knew all about talking the talk, did Al. But it wasn't enough. He had to walk the walk, and that could be bad for your health – particularly with a stone in your shoe.

CHAPTER X

THE HAMMER DROPS

Big Al indeed was losing the plot.

13 NOVEMBER 1993

VICTOR Italiano, Larry Lampert, Angelo Stromboli, Gilbert Bazooka, Luigi Costa and Little Mario Barzini were arrested on a multi-million-dollar guns and heroin raid. Codenamed Operation Hammer, the raid was led by Detective Chief Inspector Paul Holliday and involved Federal and State task forces. Also arrested was Nick ('The Greek') Postalas, Al Cologne's underling and spy. On Alfonse's orders, the treacherous Greek provided the information to police before vanishing into the witness protection programme. Beware of Greeks bearing tins.

It didn't take Bazooka long to figure out that, if the Greek gave them up, he did so on the tactical advice of Alfonse. Bazooka and his crew had lent Alfonse about $250,000 for a Russian heroin buy. The profits were to be invested in King Street property in Melbourne. Alfonse later claimed the Albanians ripped the money and tried to involve Bazooka and his crew in a gang war.

However, Gilbert found out that Alfonse had paid off a $100,000 debt to the Di Inzabella family and $100,000 to a family trust based in Milan. There was no Russian heroin deal and never had been. It was all part of Al's insolent plan to rob his fellow crooks.

While Gilbert was in prison fighting for bail – with no one yet believing his supposedly paranoid opinion re Al's treachery – Alfonse himself borrowed the cash from the Costa family to bail everyone out. Would a guilty man do such a thing? Of course not! It was all Nick the Greek's fault, Alfonse claimed, straight-faced. Some people believed him. Others almost did.

Gilbert remembered when Shane Goodfellow gave Crown evidence against Hacker Harris in the St Kilda nightclub murder. Goodfellow remained under Big Al's protection and on the payroll. Boris the Black Diamond was also facing Supreme Court on heavy heroin matters. Boris did business with Al, and Cologne had borrowed heavily from both Boris and the Chinese for a heroin deal that didn't come off. Again, the sum of money was staggering. With these thoughts as a starting point, things began to tick over in Gilbert's mind. He spoke to Gonzo and the Kindergartens. The Muratore, Italiano, Stromboli, Agillette, Lampedusa, Vasari, Brazzi, Barzini, Vittorio and Costa families also felt that something was not quite right. It was Alfonse who had told Gilbert to place Nick in such a powerful and invincible position. The Monza and Caprice families already hated Cologne and had suspected him for some time of being a transgressor and a traitor. The Monza family called Alfonse '*La Toeletta*'. You didn't have to be a language professor to work out that it meant 'the shithouse'. This was a Sicilian slang insult of the foulest kind.

'Our Calabrese *paisan*, you know,' said Poppa Nicola Stromboli to Poppa Costa over the phone. 'You know the Milano movie star. I think he's a playing the double game.' Poppa Costa listened hard.

'He has no *gratitudine*, no *riconoscenza* [thankfulness]. All the porko barstardo does is *bugia, bugia* [lie, lie],' Costa replied. 'He's a fucking juggler, borrowing money from Peter to pay Paul, then tells both men that he's been robbed. He gives police too much of the *sessanta nove*.' Stromboli laughed – 'sessanta nove' means sixty-nine, and implied that Alfonse and the police were pleasuring each other a little too hard.

'He has no honour,' said Costa, 'and no honesty. Please leave it to me, I will speak to Brazzi and arrange to see Di Inzabella.'

'Bene Grazie,' replied Stromboli and hung up the phone. He turned to Poppa Dardo and his three sons. 'Tell Mick Conforte and that Mad Charlie Hajalic that I want to see them.'

Poppa Dardo nodded and smiled.

7 OCTOBER 1994

Alfonse Cologne, Mick Conforte, Mick D'Andrea, Joe Gotto, Mad Charlie Hajalic, Carlo Di Inzabella and Ronnie Burgess sat outside the Pasta Rustica restaurant in Lygon Street, Carlton.

Di Inzabella was doing the talking: 'The shopping list is unbelievable, Al. Listen to this.'

Plates of lasagna and salad sat before the men on a large table littered with bottles of Shiraz.

Di Inzabella returned to his reading. 'The Fanucci family are in with the Stromboli clan and the Stromboli clan is in with the Dardos.'

'Ha! Ha! Ha!' snorted Alfonse.

'I don't understand,' said Mick Conforte.

'Just listen,' snapped Alfonse.

'OK,' continued Di Inzabella. 'You won't believe this. Shit! Holy Mother of God. You won't believe it. Sixty German Mauser 7.62s, and homemade 9mm sub-machine guns made by the Protestant paramilitaries in Belfast.'

'What?' said Big Al. 'Sixty of them!'

'No,' replied Di Inzabella. 'Sixty Mauser 7.62 bangers and two dozen of the 9mm subbies. OK? And Ingram 9mm sub-machine guns – at least 50 of them. Israeli-made Desert Eagle .357 magnums, .44 magnums and .50-calibre Action Express. Boxes of them. And 9mm Heckler and Koch P7 semi autos, Japanese Kyunana Shiki, 20mm model anti-tank rifles – 152 pounds of heavy-duty murder, seven-round, gas-operated, fully automatic, rare as hen's fucking teeth, Al, for Christ's sake.'

He continued, 'Browning M2 machine guns. AWP 7.62mm sniper rifles. 7.65mm Czechoslovak model 61 Scorpion sub-machine guns. Sterling 9mm L2A3 sub-machine guns.'

'Now get this,' he continued. 'One Russian-made S A 7 anti-aircraft missile, with optical aiming and infrared homing, for God's sake. A crate of old British stuff, plus 55 anti-tank rifles, a M79 grenade launcher, three Russian-made 7.62mm model Maxim machine guns, three British .303 Bren guns. Browning .50-calibre M2 machine guns. The list goes on and on. It's unbelievable, Al.'

The men sat in silence.

'Anti-aircraft guns,' said Alfonse. 'Mamma Mia. Holy fucking Madonna. We only want a dozen or so handguns. We don't want to fight World War III.'

'OK,' said Di Inzabella. 'Smith and Wesson, Rugers, Aldo Ubertis, Uberti Schofields, Colts, Walthers, Browning, Jenning, Beretta, Norinco, Springfield, Glock, Remington, Van Hee, Benilli, Pardini, Beeman, Steyr, Luger, Webley, Winchester, Takarev ...'

'OK, OK,' said Alfonse. 'Shit, how many guns have these pricks got?'

Mad Charlie Hajalic felt ill at ease. They were meant to be buying arms and ammo from the Albanians but Charlie knew there was only one crew in Australia with a stranglehold on weapons of this nature. They were all Aussies and all of them were heavily teamed up with Hacker Harris. Charlie shook his head. Big Al was indeed losing the plot. If he buys even one gun from the Albanians and lashes on the deal, he would pull the last straw. Charlie could feel Hacker's web closing in on them all.

Cherrie was 5 feet 6 inches tall in the old money, with black hair and eyes and olive skin. She was a lap dancer. She was what the Italians described as 'hot chocolate'. She had an arse that would slide on to anything erect, providing the club lighting was dim and the management even dimmer.

It was $20 for a lap dance but Cherrie had a trick that collected her an even $200 per dance. She would work up the client till the cork was about to pop and then bend down and whisper, 'Pull it out, baby.' With a quick twist and turn, amidst a club full of drunks looking on, but not paying much attention, she would slide her magnificent behind down on the rampant member and with three or four slippery slides up and down, collect his load. No one would be the wiser and all this in a crowded club. She had been sacked before for blatantly blow-jobbing clients in public, but her new trick was very hard to detect in the darkness of a strobe-lit nightclub.

Candy was the centre of attraction. Six foot tall, all tits and legs, and a Penthouse Pet-type blonde, more Las Vegas than Melbourne. But a pure professional, meaning all show, no go. Strictly look but don't touch. So, while Candy was the main attraction in the joint, hot arse Cherrie would slip and slide away on 15 or 20 stiffs a night. At 200 bucks a pop, now and again she could afford to get caught and sacked. As a gypsy dancer, she could travel from one club to another with a few nights of straight lap dancing to prove she could pull in the punters. Then she would attack them. She could knock the top of anyone in less than two seconds. She was also the girlfriend of Donny Corset, the young son of old Dino Corset, Frankie Witton's offsider. He was also a personal friend of Alfonse Cologne.

To say that Cherrie was more than a little confident was a polite understatement. However, when Alfonse raped her in a King Street club, then pistol-whipped her young boyfriend, Cherrie took the matter to Dino Corset and in turn to old Frankie Witton. Al said a thousand sorries all round but he still had a problem. Cherrie's last name was Kindergarten. Dino and Charlie, understanding that boys will be boys, forgave Big Al. But this didn't quite work with the Kindergarten family.

The Kindergartens, being the long-range chess players they were, insisted all was well and, to top it off, young Cherrie told Al that any time he wanted it he had it, knowing all the time that Big Al was going to get it anyway. Cherrie was a professional and she believed that a walking corpse always deserved one last screw.

Joe La Borchia, otherwise known as *La Piccolo Demente* ('the little lunatic'), was a Naples Italian and a Camorra man all the way back to his great-grandfather. He sat in a restaurant in Adelaide looking like thunder. Alfonse owed Joe $52,000 and the debt was long overdue. This was not good.

'*Misericordioso*,' yelled Joe in Italian, as he tended to when he got excited, which was often. 'Alfonse is the boss of the kids. He owes money. He must pay. And he expects me to cut my friendship with Hacker. Me and "Mentale" go back a long way.'

'Mentale' was Joe's pet nickname for Hacker. Again, you didn't have to be a professor of European languages to know what it meant.

'Hacker's a fucking legend,' said Joe. 'Whereas Alfonse is a mixed-race Calabrese. A Milano maggot. Alfonse I can do without. Hacker will be with me till the grave. So you can tell the fat pig bastardo

Calabrese to fuck his mother in the arse. I want my money and Hacker Harris and me are blood brothers, *capiche!*'

Johnny Conforte nodded. '*Capiche*, Joe,' he said soothingly.

'I understand that fucking De Inzabella well,' said Joe. 'We got telephones over here too, you know. The Caprice and Monza families in Sicily, they not too happy with that old rascal, as well.'

Johnny Conforte moved uneasily in his chair. Joe La Borchia (Joe the Boss) was a true rattlesnake. When Italians from all over Australia with mainland Italian and Sicilian family connections were dirty on you because you owed money to all of them, you could con Lygon Street you were Mafia until you were blue in the face. But the truth was you would either pay up or die. There was no way to warn his own family that sides must be taken, and quickly, unless they were all to finish up in the same grave.

Jas and Jody were sisters. Long, blonde and sexy to the point of tempting a saint if they ever got to Heaven, which was considered unlikely by most who knew them. The smart money said chances were they would both go to Hell for their earthly misconduct. Jas could suck the chrome off an exhaust pipe if Jody didn't get to it first. Which was why, as dancers, they were in great demand. However, while working the Melbourne clubs, they both owed their friendship and loyalty to Hacker Harris and Joe La Borchia in return for favours and kindness in the past. The sisters may have had hot pants but their friendships and hearts were blood loyal.

It is unbelievable what a man will tell a woman while his exhaust pipe is being de-chromed, and the sisters were dynamite double agents in this regard. Dead set Mata Haris, not to mention Linda Lovelace and Monica Lewinsky.

One night, Jas was busy doing exactly that for Alfonse Cologne while her sister Jody was backing up on Mad Charlie Hajalic when they heard the name Harris being mentioned along with the sum of $60,000. The name Joe La Borchia was also mentioned. The sisters couldn't believe that Al and Mad Charlie would be stupid enough to talk about a contract to have two men killed while engaging in sex in a darkened nightclub in the presence of two ladies they didn't know. But that is what methamphetamine does to people. It opens the mouths of normally silent men. Not to mention their flies and Y-fronts.

Jasmine and Jody wasted no time in alerting Hacker Harris, who was in prison, and Joe La Borchia, who wasn't, of the conversation they had overheard. Jody travelled to South Australia and Jasmine to Pentridge to pass on the information. Then, for some reason, Harris sent Jasmine to see Poppa Dardo and Poppa Brazzi. The old Albanian was very polite, thanking Jas for the message before trying to pants her – or more accurately – unpants her.

Evidently, Jody had a similar proposition put to her by Joe in South Australia. Italians, no matter who or what, could never be trusted with pussy unless it had four legs, purred and liked saucers of milk – and even then you couldn't be too sure, with some of the randy bastards. This tendency, of course, was not to be taken personally.

It was simply the nature of the beast. Chicks like Jasmine and Jody brought out the beast in every man, and it was just that the Italians were not so good at hiding their true feelings. A throbber was more a compliment than an insult and no offence was taken. But Harris and La Borchia took great offence at the message passed on to them by the helpful young ladies.

Emily Hanlon was tall, blonde and the de facto wife of Giorgo Monza. Emily was also the girlfriend of Joe La Borchia, not to mention the mother of two children to Frankie Mackenzie. She was an energetic girl.

Like half Australia's underworld, Emily was also related through marriage to the Kindergarten family. But poor Emily had a wandering eye and a pair of long legs that seemed to open whenever the word heroin was mentioned. She had met Big Alfonse Cologne and Mick Conforte in the company of Mad Charlie Hajalic at a Melbourne nightclub. To cut a long story short, Emily had ended up back at a house in Moonee Ponds in the company of Johnny Moore with a needle in her arm and several other pricks in various parts of her anatomy. Unfortunately, she had fallen in love with Big Alfonse and, via Moore, had located Cologne's unlisted telephone number.

She then made a bad mistake. She threatened to ring Al's wife, Margaret, and tell her that she was number one in Al's life. Margaret was a well-educated convent girl who was not even Italian, but love made her hook up with a flash would-be Mafia maggot like Al Cologne. She had got used to the fact that the father of her children was no gentleman, but she didn't need to have her nose rubbed in it.

The whole thing was getting out of hand. Emily was by crim standards a nice girl but a nasty drunk and even worse when on heroin. Her threat of an early-morning phone call had to be neutralised – and so did she.

So it was that Johnny Moore brought young Emily to Mick D'Andrea's club in Carlton. It was a cross between a coffee shop and a card joint. Mostly gambling went on but a little coffee was sold as well. D'Andrea ran it. Big Al owned the building. The club was perfect in that it had once been a butcher's shop and boasted a large freezer at the back that no longer worked. But once the door was shut it was semi-sound proof. It had to be.

The trouble was that, by the time Alfonse and Mick Conforte arrived, Johnny Moore and Mick D'Andrea had already dealt savagely with the girl. The only way to ease the poor girl's pain was a gentle heroin overdose. Al then ordered the remains to be disposed of. By disposal, he meant that she had to vanish for good, and not reappear floating in the Yarra River three days later.

'If you keep getting back up, the bastards will get tired of knocking you down.' – Hacker Harris.

When Hacker Harris went back inside in 1992 over another shooting, Melbourne breathed a sigh of relief as the mental case with no ears faced a charge that many thought would be his last. The bloke had pulled the gun out one too many times and, on this occasion, the bloke looking down the wrong end of the barrel was the president of a motorcycle club not averse to taking the witness stand.

Harris was seen by his enemies and their friends as a psychopathic madman who would gun you down for sixpence. The sooner he was locked away forever and a day, the better. Lygon Street went into a frenzy of near-hysterical happiness. It was like Italy had won the World Cup. They couldn't kill the big bastard but getting him locked away was nearly as good.

Half a world away, Al Cologne went into overdrive. He was never the most modest or most rational of men, and this time he was flying. 'All I want is to do what I want, when I choose, where I want with no dog putting his nose in,' he ranted. 'The Mafia is the sole property of television and the movies and the property of the imagination of mice. If mice and the local media and, for that matter, the local police and criminal world like to see me as Mafia, so be it. The bigger the lie, the more people will believe it. We put out a hit on Muratore – right outside his home in Hampton, the same way his father was shot 28 years ago. Remember Vincenzo Muratore? We pulled that off and even Di Inzabella and Stromboli and Brazzi will have to sit up and take note!'

Benny Fanucci sat at attention, listening to Al Cologne raving on. 'You see, Benny, the Mafia is what we say it is. It's an Italian thing. It's *our* thing. Fuck this Sicily bullshit. The movies invented it in the minds of the mice. So all we do is feed them the cheese and – bingo bango – you got the Mafia. Fuck the Monzas and the Caprice family and their Sicilian shit. Fucking dwarfs. We got the drugs, the guns, the muscle, the lawyers, the cops. We got every Calabrese in Melbourne convinced I'm the next best thing to the fucking Godfather. We can do what we fucking want. OK?'

Fanucci nodded. 'What about the Albanians?' he asked.

'Fuck the fucking Albanians and everyone else. That fucking Harris is gone. He will never get out. I'll outlive and outlast them all. You watch,' replied Al.

'So who will we get to do Muratore?' asked Fanucci.

'The Albanians,' laughed Alfonse. 'They will kill anyone for 10 grand.'

'Shouldn't we ask Di Inzabella first?' asked Fanucci. 'After all, he killed Muratore's father and he might get offended if we go for outside help. He might think it's his right or something.'

'Fuck Di Inzabella,' replied Alfonse. 'He's old. He's losing it. We run Melbourne. You know what? After we get Muratore knocked, we might stage them fucking dumb Albanians into knocking Di Inzabella as well.'

Alfonse Cologne sat outside a restaurant comically named the 'Aldo Moro' in Rome, Italy. He was drinking grappa and eating seafood salad. Fanucci was drinking al fuoco vino (fine wine) and eating clams. Fanucci was on his way by plane to the Punta Raisi Airport in Palermo, Sicily, to visit the Monza clan. The Monzas had invited Fanucci to a wedding at the 'Four Corners'. The main port and capital of Sicily is a beautiful city built around the centre known as La Quattro Canti – 'Four Corners'. Some 3,000 people had been invited to this wedding.

Alfonse hadn't been invited and didn't even know that Rocco Monza's daughter was getting married. This Melbourne-born Milan Calabrese false pretender was telling Fanucci that the Mafia was an invention of television. Fanucci would repeat this conversation to the Monzas. Muratore might end up dying a sudden and violent death, but Alfonse's role in it would be no secret. Fanucci knew that if he didn't repeat this conversation he would one day answer for it. That was Cologne's one fault. He had a mouth like a running tap.

'*Salut*,' said Fanucci, as he raised his glass.

'*Salut*,' replied Alfonse.

Sitting in the Roman sun, he felt like the criminal version of Julius Caesar. Who the fuck could stop him? The big man smiled and Fanucci smiled in return. Fanucci couldn't remember the last time he met an Italian with a bigger mouth and a bigger daydream than Alfonse Cologne's. This, he thought, was one Calabrese who knows everything except who should and shouldn't become his enemies – which makes him one very dumb Calabrese, indeed.

> 'A man cannot be too careful in his choice of enemies.'
> – OSCAR WILDE

Spaghetti, with an olive oil and crabmeat salad, with just a touch of garlic and tender tomato paste, is best eaten with a chilled fine grappa wine. It is a cheap Catania dish, commonly served at La Lamberto Cafe just outside the Fontanarossa Airport. Most Italians are surprised that Catania even has an airport.

'One crowded hour of glorious life is worth an age without a name,' said Joe La Borchia as if he'd thought of it first.

Fanucci nodded. Joe was a great one for quoting other people as was Big Al Cologne. He was often quoting Oscar Wilde, Napoleon,

Hitler or John F Kennedy. Hacker Harris started this bullshit off in the early 1970s. The trick with Hacker was he would invent his own quotes, and then attribute them to famous people, giving the simple-minded listener the impression he was widely read. Big Al, on the other hand, was relatively well educated and had read a few books – some without pictures.

'Never trust a Greek, a priest or a man with false teeth,' Hacker said to Alfonse one day some 20 years ago. 'Hitler said that.'

It took Big Al almost a year of research before he realised Hitler said no such thing at all.

'Never trust a one-eyed man riding a three-legged horse,' Hacker had said one other time. 'Napoleon said that.'

It was at this point that Big Al started quoting great writers, poets and politicians correctly. He was sick of being made a fool of by a no-eared mental case with the gift of the gab.

Christina and Renzo Gregori sat with them. Renzo was a short, dark-skinned Sicilian but Christina's mother came from the north of Italy and she was tall, blonde and dark-eyed, with a large set of watermelons. She was indeed quite beautiful. How Renzo fathered such a beauty was a Sicilian mystery. Christina had travelled from Melbourne for the Monza wedding and, while Big Al Cologne sat in Rome dreaming his dreams, the reality of who was really who and who would live and die and when, was being spoken of in Palermo and Catania. Don Hector Aspanis had even attended the wedding. The joke was that the would-be Mafia boy from Melbourne, the Milano Calabrese, was sitting in Rome doing business with petty crooks in Milan. He had not even been aware of the wedding, which was quite comical. He lived the Hollywood Mafia dream on the profits of his heroin money and property development. He was also of use to Di Inzabella but it had also come to light that Big Al was acting as a secret informer for certain government agencies such as the NCA and DEA, not to mention various federal and state task forces. Al played both sides of the fence but forgot it was electrified.

Drug investigations, if controlled, could be useful – providing Big Al was given certain key information that was actually misinformation. Big Al would quickly lose credibility. But as Fanucci and La Borchia agreed, Cologne had to go. Renzo nodded in agreement. Di Inzabella would have to talk to Conforte and then get Cologne to talk to Mad Charlie.

Maybe, through Charlie, they could reach out to Harris and his old crew. The Italians would set up the job but it would be carried out by others. After all, they would have to look the wife, daughters and sister in the eye at the funeral. The Italians just aren't as good at hiding their emotions as Hollywood portrays it. Everyone was in agreement. The whens and by whom and how had not yet been worked out. Oh, to be Irish because people killed one another in the street with no planning whatsoever and thought very little about it, or anything else, except perhaps the drink afterwards. But an Italian murder was an opera – and a game of chess. Much 'atenzione' had to be paid to detail long before the trigger was pulled. Tradition demanded it. This wasn't just a death. It was a political statement – and every politician's death takes much backroom planning. Everyone had to be in agreement to avoid misunderstandings and disputes later.

The whole thing was like preparing a fine Italian dish: it needed the correct amount of olive oil because you couldn't drown a man like Alfonse in vinegar. You had to sink him slowly in a bath of warm olive oil, saying 'sorry, friend' as you pushed his head under. An Italian death was almost as religious as a mass or a wedding or a funeral. First came Why? Then came How? Then Who?

'Un bicchiere di vino,' called Fanucci, and they all raised their glasses and toasted their plan.

And another nail was hammered into the Calabrese coffin.

> 'Blood and treachery are the two great blessings the Lord bestowed on the Irish people.'
> – MICHAEL COLLINS

4 MARCH 1996

Despite moves being made behind Cologne's back by the old Australian crews and his own people, the big man survived all odds. Big Al had a strange magnetism and the ability to talk his way out of death – and make a profit along the way. His ability to borrow large amounts of cash from men who didn't even trust him was all part of his personality.

Even true Mafia – the Sicilian, Napolitan and Calabrian clans – believed Cologne was 'connected'. His ongoing verbal war with Hacker Harris was all part of his psychological strategy and tactical thinking. Hacker was without doubt the most hated crim in Melbourne and, if there were no Alfonse, then Harris would be left to run wild like a fox in a hen house. Or, at least that was the impression Alfonse liked people to get.

He was America to Hacker's Russia. Without one, the other would dominate the world. Big Al was the only force in Melbourne able to control Harris, hold him at bay, kill him or keep him out of town, ran the propaganda line. The fact that Harris was in prison seemed beside the point. Harris represented blood, torture, mindless murder and general insane mayhem, while Alfonse represented some sort of order.

He had proven himself in combat by gunning down Johnny Workman in East St Kilda and proved himself as a fixer by getting away with it. By a stroke of great good fortune for Al, the DPP dropped the charges. Wicked rumours of police and political or judicial influence ran riot. The truth was the two star witnesses flew overseas thanks to Al's chequebook and the case collapsed. Big Al seemed to be the one man in Melbourne who could do as he liked when he wanted.

Al mixed with millionaires, TV and football personalities, boxers, singers and rock and roll celebrities. He was the black prince of Lygon Street, and a lot of people liked to be seen with him.

Harris, on the other hand, was a mental case who was rarely out of prison, with little more than a small following of deranged psychopaths. Yet Big Al was always a little overshadowed by this one enemy.

Al was big but, if Harris walked through the door, Cologne would call for the nappies because he would wet his pants. Even Al's friends noticed these things and muttered rumours behind Al's back. While Cologne pretended not to notice, his hatred for Harris blinded him to the true extent of the hatred he had caused to be directed towards himself.

A man must know his enemies, but Alfonse had reached the point where he could no longer tell the difference. Rumours of Harris's release from prison kept cropping up. One unnamed underworld source told the *Herald Sun* newspaper that Harris had 90 days to live. That is, if he actually was released from prison.

'I wonder what underworld source told them that?' laughed Poppa Brazzi. 'Holbrook's Worcestershire Sauce by the sounds of it. Ninety days to live, hey? They couldn't kill Hacker if they tossed holy water over him and hammered a wooden stake through his heart. You sit in Lygon Street eating seafood, pizza and drinking lemonade while the sun shines on your BMW and you make calls on your mobile phone to your lawyer. The girls may admire your $100 haircut and your $1,000 sports coat. Meanwhile, you've got one fucking popgun under the front seat of your car with six rounds of ammo and can't find anyone in Melbourne who can supply you with a box of 50 rounds and you can't hit the side of a fucking shed with a bucket full of shit in a gun fight.

'I think old no-ears will outlive us all, and especially Alfonse. Like that fucking mad Harris said, "Chequebooks don't win gang wars." Underworld source indeed,' he snorted.

CHAPTER 4

THE POPCORN GANGSTER

everyone loves a funeral.

IT'S 1997. Poppa Dardo lay dying in the Western General Hospital in Footscray. The head of the largest and most powerful criminal clan in the Melbourne Albanian criminal world had his family gathered around him. He whispered to his eldest son, 'Where is Hacker?'

Hacker wasn't there. He was still in prison, and not in Melbourne or for that matter even in the State of Victoria. After being told this, the old man called out a dying request. His son nodded. Poppa Dardo had made a blood promise in 1987 to Harris. But with one thing and another – not to mention the fact Harris couldn't seem to stop shooting people in front of witnesses – the old man had put the promise to the back of his mind. But, now, lying on his deathbed, he wanted to leave the earth with a clear heart that he owed no man a debt or an unkept promise.

So he swore his son to see to it that the promise made all those years before would be kept. So it was that, as Poppa Dardo closed his eyes for the last time, the last nail was hammered into the Calabrese coffin. The last request of a dying man could not, and would not, be ignored. As the family left the hospital, one son spoke to another. 'Tell Conforte I want to see him and, while you're at it, arrange a meeting with Charlie Hajalic.'

'Who's Al running with these days?' asked the eldest son.

The younger brother replied, 'Moore and old Kindergarten.'

'Good,' said the elder son. 'Forget Moore. Gilbert and his crew want him. Arrange a meeting with Mumbles. I will go and see Di Inzabella myself. The time has come.'

'What time has come?' asked young Sally, Poppa Dardo's granddaughter.

'When a man dies, his debts must be paid and his wishes obeyed. That's what Poppa Dardo asked for,' the eldest son answered.

'Oh,' said Sally, still puzzled.

Perth, 1997. Tony Capone was the eldest and most powerful member of the Calabrian crime family from Melbourne, but he wasn't the only Tony Capone by a long shot. The clan had the comic habit of naming every second male in the extended family 'Tony', so that sons, brothers and uncles all answered to the same name. This created trouble for the BCI, ABCI, NCA and the Federal Police, especially when tapping phones. They all spoke in Italian when on the phone and, to white-bread Aussie coppers, they all sounded alike – like tough Italians with bad attitudes.

The cops listened into these phone conversations with growing bewilderment – they were between men named Tony about men named Tony. But, in reality, the 'person of interest' was little fat Tony, a bull-necked, barrel-chested killer who, with heroin money, had established himself as one of the most powerful criminal identities in Western Australia. This was the Tony the police were particularly interested in.

There had been some interesting conversations in certain Italian circles. Di Inzabella had given the nod and the Albanians had requested he speak with all other Calabrese clans regarding the matter of Cologne.

The only fly in the pie was the one, but not only, Tony Capone. A one-time legend in Melbourne, he – together with Machine Gun Charlie, Frankie Longnose, Brian and Les Kane, Happy Allard, Charlie Witton, Jackie Twist and others – had given Big Mick Conforte and Al Cologne their start.

In wealth and power, not to mention connections, Tony Capone and his clan, who spread from Western to South Australia to Victoria, could not be ignored. It was Cologne's supposedly great friendship with the shadowy Capone that was his greatest weapon. Cologne counted on the fact that Capone was the one, if push came to shove, who could out-gun and override Di Inzabella, Stromboli, Muratore, Italiano, Agillette, Fanucci, Gatto, D'Andrea, Bazooka, Lampedusa, Vasari, Brazzi, Monza, Vittorio and Barzini. The whole lot, in others words. He didn't have the full house but he was convinced he held the ace in the pack.

Capone was smart in that he was a Calabrese who actually did do big business with the Sicilians, rather than just talk about it. He had even married a Sicilian in Sicily. Then, in South Australia, he married a blonde model – shrugging off the small matter of bigamy. The only man Capone had no hold over was Joe La Borchia and so it was Joe who spoke to Capone.

Tony had lent Al Cologne $100,000 for legal bills and had never been repaid. Capone also hated Harris. So any mention of the Albanians acting against Cologne to repay a debt for Harris could not be mentioned. It was the news that Moore had introduced Cologne to methamphetamines that sent Capone round the twist.

After the death of his mother and father, Big Al had taken to secretly using speed – firstly to lose weight, then to party at night. Capone hated junkies. Any use of drugs outraged him. The fact that he sold millions of dollars' worth of heroin and speed was beside the point. His attitude was, if Big Al was using powders, then fuck him. Whether or not Al really was a junkie was Harris's little secret. After all, it was Hacker who started the rumour in the first place. But, as Big Al was fond of saying, 'The bigger the lie, the more people will believe it.'

'*Triplo concentrato di pomodoro*,' muttered Alfonse to himself. Or at least it sounded something like that. Written Italian was never the author's strong point – '*Beretta*' being about the only Italian word he spells with any confidence. But, I digress ... Al was making an olive oil, onion and garlic sauce. Beside him was the Hot English Mustard, his secret weapon. He never told anyone that the fire in his dishes came from this particular condiment. Big Al claimed to be not only an intellectual, but also a great cook. No Italian would ever admit to adding a tablespoon of Hot English Mustard to any dish. But the English had created a mustard hotter than the devil's bottom. Alfonse would invent his own dishes, then claim it was his mother's or grandmother's old secret passed on to him.

Nine times out of ten, a dog wouldn't eat it. But, tonight, his good friend and great legal, political and social adviser was coming to dinner. The fridge was full of French champagne, but the puzzle for Al was whether the delicate tongue of his adviser would pick up on the fact that a Calabrese dish had been laced with Hot English Mustard. Even if she did, she was not to know that this was a trick that had been used in Lygon Street pizza parlours for years, always in secret.

Al's own mother had introduced him to Hot English Mustard as a child. He now threw it around the kitchen so much that just getting near some of his creations made your eyes water. Hmmm! thought Al. Will I add the Calabrese fire to this truly home-cooked Italian dish in the usual way? Yes! Why not? How far he had come. One night he was out with the crew smashing people with billiard cues. The next night he was cooking up a storm for a respected member of Melbourne society.

Terry Domican was on the phone to him from New South Wales regularly. Big fucking business. Tony Capone loved him. Jimmy Kizon was up his arse every weekend. Alfonse mixed with the glitterati and the gutter with ease. One night, the kick-boxing, the next the ballet. It was all the same to him.

Easy on the garlic, thought Al. But then again, who would notice the garlic amid the mustard? His mind turned to Harris. I wonder what that mental case had for dinner tonight in his cell. No matter. That's where the mad dog belongs, in a cage for life.

The newspapers and media seemed to have a love and hate affair with Harris. Alfonse couldn't read a paper or turn on the television without hearing Hacker Harris laughing at him. Al nodded to himself. Conforte was right. Harris played the media like a fine violin. The whole country saw him as little more than a scallywag comic and seemed to forgive him the river of blood he had swum in all his life. Harris this, Harris that, the no-eared mental case won't stop. Alfonse continued his cooking. I'll outlive you fat boy, he thought, adding a couple of dollops of cream to the sauce. He was quoting what Hacker had said to him so many years ago.

'Fuck it,' said Alfonse, 'too much mustard.'

Sometimes in the dead of night, Big Al dreamed of Hacker Harris and wondered what the two of them could have achieved had they been friends rather than enemies. After all, they did start as mates.

'Do it now. Not tomorrow. Not yesterday. *Now!*' Joe La Borchia stood screaming down the telephone.

Joe was in the Da Renato Restaurant in Palermo, Sicily, and was talking long distance to Poppa Di Inzabella himself. Di Inzabella put the phone down and made a call to Mick Conforte.

'Mick,' said Di Inzabella, 'it's time to have a talk to Charlie. Tell Charlie if he can fix it then he can have half. I'm sorry, Mick. But it all needs to be sorted. No bullshit. Morto. Just talk. But take Charlie, the Albanian, and the blue-eyed man. The Albanian will do the talking. Trust me, Mick. Al can come out of this OK if you can fix it. Talk to Mumbles but sort it out, for Christ's sake. It's all gone too far. The Calabrese has to bow out with grace and allow others to continue. Set up the meeting. You have my word, Mick. No tricks. Just talk. Al knows this has been coming. If he agrees, all debts are forgotten and he goes on the company pension list. He won't suffer money wise. Set it up please, Mick. One more phone call from Sicily and they will have me hit. Al doesn't understand. It's all gone too far. This isn't one of Hacker Harris's books.'

'OK,' said Mick before hanging up the phone.

It all came back to Mick setting up a meeting with men who had known Hacker Harris for over 20 years. You didn't need to be a brain surgeon to figure out who had spun this web. But, life must go on and, to continue, a little death must happen now and again.

Conforte shrugged. 'Fuck Al. He wanted to party. Now he has to rock and roll.'

10 JANUARY 1998

Mick Conforte's car was parked in front of Mad Charlie Hajalic's home in South Caulfield. Charlie was the only man in Melbourne who could talk to not only the Albanians but also Harris's old crew as the work that needed to be done could not be done by an Italian. There would, after all, be a funeral to attend. However, Big Mick kept telling himself that it was just talk. Talk, talk.

Di Inzabella had already been on the phone to Charlie and Charlie knew that this would be the last talk. As Mick sat in Charlie's bedroom, he began to cry. It was all too much for Conforte. Talk, he keep telling himself. Just a talk. Di Inzabella talked to people in his own home or out in the backyard. Conforte didn't want to admit it. But he knew in his heart that this talk would be the last one for his old friend Alfonse. While Mick sat in Charlie's bedroom, Geoff Kindergarten rang. Then there were three phone calls from the Albanians. After that, Charlie made two cryptic phone calls. Mick could smell the shadow of Hacker Harris in the room. After all, hadn't Mad Charlie and Hacker grown up together? Just as Mick and Alfonse had done. '*Mi spiace*, Alfonse [I'm sorry, Alfonse],' said Mick to himself.

> 'You tell people you're in the Mafia, you make fucking damn sure you're a fucking Sicilian.'
> – JOE PESCI

In the end, you can be as mobbed up, plugged in, connected, crewed up, teamed up and as Italian as Mussolini's bumhole, but, if you're not a full-blood Sicilian, then you're just another *ipocrita* (hypocrite). A fucking *allucinazione* (hallucination). You can wear all the Italian suits you like and stuff your face with pizza and chatter in Italian with your crew, friends and even hangers-on. Even kid the newspapers and the police that Robert De Niro is alive and well, living in fucking Templestowe and eating fettuccine and salad in Lygon Street. But in the end it is only that – an hallucination. Many men live out a criminal hallucination. But no man does it with the pomp and style of the Italian.

Meanwhile, in Melbourne, Mick Conforte and Alfonse Cologne (nicknamed Al Cologne) were at Happy Allards' two-up game in Port Melbourne. It was one of the many places where they were paid protection money. Jesus, Hollywood has spent billions scaring the shit out of the world with the word Mafia. Any Italian criminal or crew of criminals would be totally stupid not to take full advantage of it. So I guess they cannot be blamed for stepping into the shoes already made for them. Unfortunately, now and again, these nitwits piss off a real Sicilian, a true Mafia guy, just like in the movies.

These peanut brains are supposed to be loved and respected yet when they are killed not one shot is fired in return. Why no fire? Because the poor dead fool never was Mafia to begin with. It takes the nod from one Sicilian and the rest of the make-believe boys will fall into line. After all they have spent their lives creating their own dreams under the shadow of the Sicilian *armaiuolo* (gunsmith). Dream merchants can't fight back because their whole world is make-believe. Their image is illusion, heroin, methamphetamine, prostitution, gambling, rar, rar, rar! That's all real to them but shoot one of the monkeys and see what happens. A thousand threats along with a thousand flowers and tears or death notices and then fucking nothing.

> 'Life is the biggest movie of them all.
> The only problem is, you only get to see it once.'
> – MARTIN SCORSESE.

'Mick will get you in. Mumbles will leave the gate open and turn off the security system. Just remember to turn the alarm back as you leave,' instructed Charlie.

The Albanian replied, 'You're coming with us.'

Charlie was taken aback by this. He was a middleman. He always had been. Neither a Mister Little or Big. He just put the two together. Charlie was a 'fixer' who preferred never to soil his hands. The last time he tried such a game he had been shot in the guts at the front of his own home. Appalled, he replied, 'No, I'm out of it.'

The Albanian stared hard at Charlie. 'You've been playing fucking gangster all your life. You betray Hacker to go with Al. Hacker was your dearest friend. Now you want to set up the biggest hit in Melbourne and keep your fucking hands clean. You know the man with Blue Eyes doesn't like you. Rod Attard is in with Blue Eyes. They are all old crew members of Hacker. My father loved Hacker. Conforte will set it all up. La Borchia flew to Sicily to see Monza. My own family has talked to every Calabrese family and crew in Melbourne. They all know that Monza gave the nod. Shit, even Capone in Western Australia has said he will ignore it. I'm telling you now, Charlie, for once in your life, show some dash. You've made your money. You've done well. The only man with any guts in this town has spent half his life in prison while the "*festivo*" boys have laughed'. The Albanian used an old *scarchi* slang word meaning festival or party boys. 'If you don't come, Charlie, I swear Monza will think you're a fucking weak "*furetto*" [ferret].'

Charlie was quickly picking up the point. The Albanian had been on the phone with Monza personally. Hadn't Hacker Harris gone to school in Thomastown with some of the young Monza boys? Who was pulling the strings? Not Conforte. Certainly not the Albanian. Blue Eyes did as he was told. Poppa Dardo was dead. Someone was still doing the thinking. Mumbles, yes, but he wouldn't knowingly involve Hacker's old crew and demand Charlie attend. Mumbles always thought Hacker was a nutcase and wouldn't have anything to do with him (or so the story went). But then again, with Hacker, what story could be believed?

His art was psychological warfare combined with combat strategy. You could shoot someone and not even know Harris had manipulated you into it. The old chess player had killed more people from his prison cell than anyone in Australia. Charlie had no way out. Harris worked on old loyalties and favours, not cash. He did you a favour today, but expected you to do one tomorrow.

Charlie knew that the demand that he attend at the home of Alfonse was Hacker's payback for Charlie not backing him in 1987 against Cologne. Hacker had put it together meticulously. When it was done, there would be so many in Melbourne to blame, but no one would be held accountable. '*Capiche*,' said Charlie to himself. At last he understood. He didn't like it but he had to admire it.

'All I want to do is live longer than my enemies.' – Hacker Harris.

Up to a 1,000 people crowded into the old Gothic-style St Mary's Star of the Sea Catholic church in West Melbourne for Big Al's funeral. Crowds spilled into the gardens surrounding the church. The crowd waited patiently through Pavarotti's 'Nessum Dorma' before taking Communion. As they queued in line before the coffin bearing a photo of the man it contained, the image seemed like that of a saint. The song 'Ave Maria' broke the silence.

One man stood in the background. Benito Monza had sent him

from Sicily 'to ensure the turd was flushed'. Next to him stood Joe La Borchia. The presence of these two men and the fact that Tony Capone didn't even attend, along with the Muratore, Italiano, Agillette, Stromboli or Di Inzabella clans, reinforced that the threats made at the grave about the plot already being dug for the man or men who had perpetrated the killing were hollow. Words made by foolish and emotional children. He may not have been in the Mafia, but this Calabrese had made sure his funeral was like that of a 'Boss'. As Bobby Pantano sang 'Ave Maria', the police and media filmed the show. After all, it was a major production. Italian funerals are like Italian food. As Shakespeare said, 'Much ado about nothing.'

Harris had successfully put a misinformation campaign in place some 12 months before the body of the deceased hit the floor. This was one jigsaw the cops would never work out. None of the Italians at the funeral even wanted it analysed either. With Big Al gone, there was room for everyone on the ladder to step up a rung. Detective Chief Inspector Rod Coleman spoke to Charlie Ford and Big Jim Reeves. 'It's no use us being drawn into speculation, boys. It's all guesswork. Everyone blames Hacker Harris. He's like fucking Ned Kelly. Each time a bloody horse goes missing, blame it on the Kelly gang.'

'What about Mumbles?' asked Rod.

'Nah,' said Charlie. 'He's on our side. He swears he knew fuck all.'

'What about Mad Charlie and the rest of Hacker's old crew?'

'Nah,' replied Charlie Ford. 'Foul slander and gossip. It was an Italian thing. No outsiders involved.'

'Hmm!' mused Rod. 'I thought so.'

Charlie patted Rod on the back. 'Fuck it, mate. One more dead maggot. Don't take it personally.'

Rod looked up. 'Personally. Shit, Charlie. I couldn't give a damn. But, if I could link Harris with it, we'd get that nut away forever.'

Charlie laughed. 'Harris is worth his weight in bullets, Rod. Without a counterweight. A counter-brilliance. The bloody Italians would run the lot. Shit, Banjo Paterson would turn in his grave.'

Rod walked away, realising that on this investigation he was alone. Not even his fellow officers would lend a hand and, to be fair, why should they? Only two criminals in Melbourne history had ever been given a ticket to ride an official police 'blind eye': Dennis Allan and Hacker Harris. Allan died from heart disease – which was a surprise to those who knew him as they thought he didn't have one. Harris survived – his was made of stone. Bluestone. You got to have a bit of clout to get that and Harris got his from the armed robbers. Allan was only a second-string player protected by Brian Paul and his motley crew. Hacker had half the St Kilda Road complex backing him in the 1987 war. Rod knew he was up against it trying to solve this one.

For a start, he felt he was the only man not in on the joke. The fucking Calabrians told lies and the Sicilians wouldn't tell you anything at all. Then you had Harris spreading total rubbish from one end of town to another from a prison cell. The entire thing was impossible.

Outside the church, the BMWs and Mercedes circled like sharks. A black Cadillac hearse stood at the ready festooned with wreaths. Old Italian men with young blondes on their arms, tough thugs and muscled brutes all wearing slip-ons, sunglasses and gold jewellery stood together that day. But not out of friendship.

Melbourne is a cross between America's New York and London's East End. It is an Australian criminal city like no other in the country. Everyone loves a funeral. Except Harris, who never attended funerals or left death notices unless some smartarse put one in for him using his name.

'Look at this shower of shit,' said La Borchia to Monza. 'He lived like a fucking movie and now he wants to die like one. It's a wonder they don't sell popcorn in the church. That's all Al was. A popcorn gangster.'

Monza smiled. 'Hear the angry talk?' whispered Monza. 'They want to kill everyone. If they fire one shot in return, you can fuck me, Joe. Look at these weak mice. If the television cameras weren't across the road, half these dogs wouldn't be here.'

'That's Melbourne,' said Joe.

They love tradition. The big occasions – Anzac Day, the Grand Final, the Melbourne Cup and a pretend gangster's funeral.

'Crocodile tears, most of the time.' Monza nodded. 'Counting me, Joe, there are only seven Sicilians at the whole funeral and six of them are shopkeepers. So much for Mister fucking Mafia.'

Joe couldn't control his laughter so he put his hands over his face and pretended to cry. This caused some in the gathering to turn their heads, but Monza's hard face made them turn away just as quickly.

As the congregation filed out of the church, an old Italian walked up to Joe. 'Why, Joe? Why they do this? Poor Alfonse, his wife, his daughters. I knew his father. He was a good man. Alfonse not Mafia. I know him since he "*bambino*".'

Joe looked at the old man and then at Monza. With a wink he replied, 'Maybe Jesus wanted him for a sunbeam.'

Tasmania POLICE

COMMISSIONER'S OFFICE
47 Liverpool Street Hobart
[GPO Box 308C]
HOBART TAS 7001
Phone   (03) 6230 2111
Fax   (03) 6230 2117

Our Ref:

Your Ref:

Enquiries:

6 June 2000

Mr M B Read
PO Box 122
RICHMOND   TAS 7025

Dear Mr Read

Thank you for your letter of 2 June 2000 in which you request me to reconsider the decision to prohibit you from possessing a firearm.

I have forwarded your correspondence to our Firearms Registry for consideration.

I shall notify you when a decision in regard to your request has been made.

Yours sincerely

R McCreadie
COMMISSIONER OF POLICE

The battle continues …